Do Less Better

Do Less Better

The Power of Strategic Sacrifice in a Complex World

John R. Bell

First published in 2014 by
PALGRAVE MACMILLAN®
in the United States—a division of St. Martin's Press LLC,
175 Fifth Avenue, New York, NY 10010.

Where this book is distributed in the UK, Europe and the rest of the world,
this is by Palgrave Macmillan, a division of Macmillan Publishers Limited,
registered in England, company number 785998, of Houndmills,
Basingstoke, Hampshire RG21 6XS.

Palgrave Macmillan is the global academic imprint of the above companies
and has companies and representatives throughout the world.

Palgrave® and Macmillan® are registered trademarks in the United States,
the United Kingdom, Europe and other countries.

ISBN: 978–1–137–45277–1

Library of Congress Cataloging-in-Publication Data

Bell, John Richard.
    Do less better : the power of strategic sacrifice in a complex world /
John Richard Bell.
      pages cm
    ISBN 978–1–137–45277–1 (hardback)
    ISBN 1–137–45277–3 ()
      1. Strategic planning. 2. Organizational change. 3. Success in business.
    I. Title.

HD30.28.B4496 2015
658.4'012—dc23   2014024353

A catalogue record of the book is available from the British Library.

Design by Newgen Knowledge Works (P) Ltd., Chennai, India.

First edition: December 2014

10 9 8 7 6 5 4 3 2 1

This book is dedicated to those
who believe that
big ideas trump big budgets

Contents

List of Figure and Tables   ix

Introduction   1

1 Accept the Short-term Pain   11

2 The Steel and Steal of Strategic Sacrifice   35

3 Your Leadership Reality Check   57

4 The Urgency for Action   87

5 Think Like an Entrepreneur   109

6 KISS Is Not a Rock Band   133

7 Bastions of Branding   155

8 Fewer, Better People Doing Less, Better   175

9 Regrets... I've Had a Few   199

Acknowledgments   213

Notes   215

Index   221

Figure and Tables

Figure

4.1   The Crisis Curve: Urgency for Action   94

Tables

1.1   1994/95 Coca-Cola and PepsiCo Sales, Profit, and Market Value   20

1.2   2013 Coca-Cola and PepsiCo Sales, Profit, and Market Value   20

1.3   7 Time-Honored P&G Darlings Killed or Sold   32

8.1   British Columbia Lottery Revenue, Profit and Headcount   179

Introduction

I magine that you are the newly hired CEO of a troubled multi-food company in desperate need of a turnaround. Here are just a few characteristics of the Gordian knot you are faced with untangling:

1. Your sales are in decline. Annual turnover is $75 million. Four consecutive years of red ink amount to $20 million. Those losses are deepening.
2. The company is a regional player, participating in ten product categories with no competitive advantage and high operating costs. One of those categories accounts for almost half of all sales.
3. The company's offerings exceed a thousand stock keeping units, exacerbating inventory costs and negative cash flows.
4. The vast majority of your 500+ employee workforce is unionized, and their hourly wages surpass those of the competition by 15 percent.
5. The shareholders are kicking in cash to keep the operation afloat, but their patience is waning. Your predecessor was out the door after only 18 months on the job.

That should be adequate information to raise two questions in your mind—"What was I thinking when I accepted this job?" and "How the hell am I going to fix this mess?" Inevitably, you will rack your brain trying to figure out how to stop the bleeding. The top line is the place where most chief executives start—how can you generate more sales? I'll venture a guess that you will consider expanding to new geographies, adding more products and categories, and line-extending your brands. You will also look at reducing your cost structure and pinpointing problems specific to each product group, all in an effort to create scale economies and erase the red ink. I am betting that your rectification plan will mirror that of your failed predecessor. In other words, you will embark on doing more of the same, but you will be determined to do it better.

You are kidding yourself.

Strategically, *doing more of the same...better* is a pathway to incremental improvement, at best. Incremental improvement is never enough to fix strategically weak companies like the one I have described.

What *should* you do? Is it possible that by actually *doing less...better*, you might improve the odds of clawing your way out the quicksand? Your shareholders and your stakeholders will not look at this ploy with enthusiasm because it is difficult for them to comprehend how *doing less* can possibly rectify an enterprise that surely needs to do *more*.

Strange as it may sound, sacrifice in the right places is often the answer and the springboard for the long-term prosperity for you and your company. I will put it this way—the sacrifice *you* make determines your fate.

The troubled company I have depicted is not fictitious. At one time it operated as Nabob Foods, the Canadian subsidiary of global coffee and chocolate maker Jacobs Suchard. During the dreary days of red ink, I served as vice-president of marketing, eventually ascending to the corner office. To escape the jaws of defeat, our young management team (most of us were in our early 30s) made several tough calls. But the most difficult and painful decisions didn't come until we accepted the unavoidable truth that we could not survive by continuing to operate as a multi-food company competing against the likes of Kraft and Nestlé—healthy, wealthy companies ten times our size. Something had to go.

Our first move was to terminate the six poorest-performing product lines within our ten-category portfolio. We looked at this as a tough strategic choice, but there was more to it than that. It was also a tough sacrifice. Tough sacrifices are about *you*. They claw at your emotions because they require that you do something that you don't want to do. Tough sacrifices rob you of sleep, sober your disposition, heighten your stress, and choke your patience on the littlest things in life.

We had made the right call, but we had failed to sacrifice enough. The termination of these product lines and brands freed up some cash, but the river of red continued to gush. Another gut-wrenching time was upon us. We believed that our branded coffee business, Western Canada's leader in retail market share, offered the best shot at a future. To realize that opportunity and to survive, we would have to make a greater sacrifice. We didn't want to do it, but we would have to divest two of the remaining sacred cows, two product lines with significant sales revenue and growth potential. What's more, these products occupied the number two brand positions in their respective markets. By killing these darlings, our $75 million company would be a shadow of its former self—down to only 2 categories, 35 stock keeping units, 200 employees, and just $50 million in sales.

I'm guessing that you were struck by the $25 million plunge in sales far more than you were by the massive drop in employment. So were we, until it came time to fire the majority of the workforce. When a leader severs the heads of 300 faceless workers in a distant plant, and collects board accolades for doing so, the bloodletting isn't that difficult. Firing confidants as well as loyal and long-termers is another matter. So is purposely shrinking revenue in the short term that you know will have to be augmented—not to mention that leading a smaller, slimmed down company represents a loss in prestige for most executives. In the pages to follow, you will hear more about this turnaround, as well as the corporate futures of some of the people involved and the impact this experience had on me for the remainder of my career. At this point, I will cut to the chase. The result of our sacrifices, large and small, became legendary within the Canadian consumer packaged goods industry.

You see, we gave up something of value (brands and businesses worth $25 million in sales) for the sake of other considerations. That is the essence of sacrifice. A strategic focus on the Nabob coffee brand with a tea line designated as a cash flow generator allowed us to give our limited funds, our know-how, and our full attention to one category. Determining unique consumer benefits from new vacuum packaging technology, we exponentially grew market share in existing markets and established a powerful presence in virgin territories to become the leading coffee brand in the nation. In just three years, our sales reached $100 million (95% in coffee, 5% in tea), and by the time we sold the company to Kraft for much more than that, the Nabob Coffee Company had delivered 13 uninterrupted years of venerable earnings growth and maintained its position as market leader.

People understand how we propelled our coffee business to 27 percent of the national market, but they still ask how we managed to sustain an advantage against giant multinationals Kraft and Nestlé. My answer may surprise you, and it is a critical spoke in the specialist strategy—beyond the technology advantages and clever advertising, category know-how reigned supreme. Consider this: the brain capacity of these giants was spread over dozens of businesses with dozens of problems (and opportunities). We gave 100 percent of our blood, sweat, and tears to one business, coffee. Can you feel my passion?

Oh, and there is one more thing. A wise man once said, "If it ain't broke, don't fix it." When it comes to business, a wiser man went on to say, "Fix it before it breaks." Whether you are a CEO, a social media marketer, an accountant, or a production line supervisor, appreciate that the toughest sacrifices are the ones you make when everything is hunky dory. This separates builders from bankers. Personal sacrifice is the strategic leadership component that ensures sustainability.

The divestment of Jacobs Suchard's international assets to Kraft was consummated in 1990, with the exclusion of Chicago candymaker Brach's, Van Houten Chocolate, and the North American coffee business. The coffee and chocolate operation that I headed reverted back to its original nomenclature, Nabob Foods, under the ownership of the Jacobs family, but minus several premium European chocolate brands such as Toblerone, Milka, and Cote D'Or that had gone over to Kraft in the sale.

After three years of continued success as a focused independent, once more, Kraft came knocking. This time, the great grandnephew of Jacobs Suchard's founder succumbed to the deep pockets of the archenemy I had fought tooth and nail for 17 years. Shortly after the acquisition, I stepped down on my own accord. I should have been ecstatic with my golden handshake, but to me it was a poison pill that was hard to swallow. That business had become a part of me—it was more than a job. So were the devoted people who worked alongside me, people who willfully sacrificed their blood, sweat, and tears to make this company their pride and joy, and the envy of the industry.

At 47 years old, I was too young to walk away from business. Would my panacea be a return to the C-suite, a start-up, or a completely different career path? Jumping back into the corner office seemed the obvious solution. But, no, I chose a transitory role. Despite my firmly held belief that the last thing the world needed was another consultant, I made some calls to my executive network and hung up a shingle. In my mind, a year of consulting in my niche of "strategic restructuring" at the executive level would give me the time to determine how I might reacquire my sense of purpose. A year of consulting became ten on a full-time basis, and another nine as a part-timer. By the time

I slipped into the CEO afterlife for good, I'd counseled some of the world's leading consumer goods organizations, a blue chip list of two dozen clients such Campbell's Soup, Anheuser-Busch InBev, Pfizer, Starbucks, and Maple Leaf Foods.

My role as the outside "hired hand" confirmed my beliefs about leadership and strategy. More importantly, it opened my eyes to the glaring and repeated errors made by dwellers of the C-suite and their understudies. At the outset of most assignments, troubled leaders and managers spoke of the issues and the success factors of their departments, their company, and their industry. I say "troubled" because people rarely call in consultants unless there's a problem they can't or don't want to fix themselves. Herein lay my renewed purpose, but indeed a decidedly different one.

Three years ago, I began penning business blogs in which I shared personal reflections and contemporary views on the state of leadership, strategy, and marketing. I've worked in a variety of businesses and managed to survive several recessions before and after the tech phenomenon. The CEOafterlife.com became the catch basin and the conduit to carry these musings to leaders and managers caught in the tangled knots of complexity, uncertainty, and information overload. Seemingly, I'm not yesterday's man. You can call 400,000+ website hits a vanity indicator, but to me that number suggests my insights have struck a chord with an audience.

This would not have been possible had I not kept pace with the pulse of the new economy of the information age. Equally important, as it relates to the insights in this book, is the unique opportunity the serenity of the CEO afterlife affords—the luxury of stepping back from the day-to-day to ponder the present-day pertinence of the stratagems that worked for me in the line of fire, and more recently as an advisor to other CEOs and CMOs. Several of these past practices remain intact, ready to be unbridled, ready to address the issues that inhibit business performance in the twenty-first century. Some require significant adaptation. Others ought to be buried in the resting place of turntables, Betamax players, boom boxes, and Walkmans.

I did not write the book that is in your hands to add another "quick-fix" solution to the litany of business paperbacks lining book store shelves. Yes, you are guaranteed to find oodles of old tricks for new dogs in its pages, but only those that will help simplify your life and improve your performance as a leader and manager in an increasingly complex world.

I'm going to say a lot about killing darlings, culling the herd, and pruning the garden over the next couple of hundred pages. Reference to *killing your darlings* comes from the literary world—a phrase commonly attributed to William Faulkner. However, in my research of the term, I learned that it was literary critic Arthur Quiller-Couch who originally advised authors to avoid "extraneous ornamentation." Quiller-Couch put it this way: "Whenever you feel an impulse to perpetrate a piece of exceptionally fine writing, obey it whole-heartedly and delete it before sending your manuscripts to press. Murder your darlings."

Bad writing and bad business are easy to cut. But just like novelists and poets, business leaders also have their darlings and sacred cows, and sometimes they have to be murdered.

Recognizing that business models change and so do consumer behaviors, I include several case studies to support the immutable premise that the right kinds of sacrifice disable complexity and pave a clearer path to the Promised Land. The starting place is the big picture itself. No matter when, where, or how a company competes, leadership is still the heart, culture is the soul, and strategy is the backbone of the organization. Sacrifice is the hidden power within each.

Not so long ago, this book's target audience would have been occupants of the "ivory tower," today's C-suite. The ivory tower used to be considered the enterprise's brain. The masses below the brain were the muscle; the muscle never got to see the brain's intricate mosaic or contribute to the big picture. There is no place for this modus operandi in today's world of business.

More than ever before, young managers are sponges for relevant commentary on leadership, strategy, and culture. Whether you are a business student, social media marketer, brand manager, human resource practitioner, management consultant, or C-suite executive, this book will give you a deeper understanding of how focus and sacrifice sidestep the detours of complication that block the stairway to your dreams.

CHAPTER 1

Accept the Short-term Pain

I'm willing to bet that your "to-do" list reflects as many as a dozen priorities. Sure, there are everyday tasks that have to be done to keep things humming, but how many of those priority projects are accomplishing medium- to long-term goals? How many take you away from those goals, but you would feel weird setting them aside? Why are you allowing this list to keep you from doing the most important things really well?

Complexity is in the eye of the beholder. To you and me, astrophysics is a complex discipline, but to Stephen Hawking, it is not. He made his discoveries by tackling one big problem at a time. When human beings are forced to deal with a certain state of affairs that is highly complex, such as writing, or even trying to comprehend a 1,000-page legislative bill, some will deal with convoluted minutiae better than do others. People who engage in complex situations fall into two categories: those who accept complexity as a fact of life and work with it, and those who fight it every inch of the way, eager to rectify it. I'm in the latter camp; I have never been good at managing complexity. This explains why I am such an advocate of simplicity. This is how I've rolled since I was a kid.

Complexity has many definitions. In my mind, excessive complication says it best. Okay, I might have simplified that a touch. That was intentional—simplification and clarity are the cornerstone of this book. Simplicity's archenemy lurks everywhere. In business alone, there are hundreds of reasons why ambiguity and complexity rear their ugly heads to complicate your professional life—some of these reasons are externally driven, but most are self-created—maybe not by you, but by people above and/or before you. Beyond the black hole of information technology and turbulent markets and economies is a long list of self-imposed phenomena, beginning with swollen management structures and the insatiable human desire to add products, services, staff, projects, and processes in the name of strategic opportunity.

I recently read that when business complexity increases, managerial complexity isn't too far behind. You can also say that when management complexity increases, business complexity isn't far behind. Both scenarios are unnecessary. The theory of breaking down complicated businesses into digestible bites has been around for a long time. Multiproduct companies in various markets that appreciate this organizational strategy succeed by narrowing their businesses into manageable units. We used to call them strategic business units (SBUs), that is, individual profit centers that focus on product offerings and market segments. General Electric and Procter & Gamble (P&G) continue to do this well.

Decisions ought to be made with the same haste in big businesses as in small ones. Yes, I know this sounds utopian, but as a goal, it can be a game changer. There are countless examples of companies that have cut through the quagmires of complexity and emerged with renewed nimbleness. Some of these companies are the largest on the planet. At the outset, someone had the will to stamp out the complexity virus. That resolve must come from the top, but successful implementation and execution (pardon the pun) will elude even the most zealous simpliphyte if the rest of the organization does not buy into the notion of transformational change.

Q: Assuming corporate leaders have the will to change, how on earth do they garner the support of their followers to make the change?

A: When they convince the entire team that focus and sacrifice are in each person's best interest because they represent everyone's roadmap to a better place. The better place is the leader's vision. Rational acceptance is not enough. People must accept the notion emotionally.

Within their wide-ranging mandate, chief executive officers (CEOs) in particular are taxed with the ongoing challenge of delivering superior earnings today, driving up stock prices today, and setting the best course for their company's brighter tomorrow while not screwing up today. This doesn't come easy; they all face problems, and with every problem, there must be a solution. They speak of scale, of critical mass, of innovation, of efficiencies, of focus, of rightsizing (that always means "downsizing") and on, and on, and on. They nod to the importance and the success of focusing efforts, but few simplify. Few think about, or measure ROE. In this case, ROE is not return of equity. It stands for return on *effort*.

Thanks to the good work of the UK management consulting firm Simplicity, we now know that the cost of complexity is quantifiable. Complexity wastes needless time and adds billions of dollars to cost structures around the globe. The cost of this epidemic to the 200 biggest companies on the globe is estimated at 10.2 percent of their annual profits—in cold hard cash, $237 billion dollars in earnings before interest, taxes, depreciation, and amortization (EBITDA).[1] That's one heck of a consequence. These are inefficiency costs that come from overexpanding and alienating customers, confusing employees, and causing cultural stress that inhibits the contentment that every person deserves in his or her place of work. Reality check: throughout the course of your working life, you will spend roughly one-half of your conscious hours on the job. That amounts to a lot of working years. Don't you think you owe it to yourself to enjoy your job, the people with whom you work, and the place in which you ply your trade?

To the plethora of leaders and managers who view complexity as an uncontrollable fact of life, I ask whether your viewpoint is the ramification of a twenty-first-century business environment that doesn't allow focus, or is it that human beings can't figure out how to do less, better? It's not as though today's young leaders and managers do not understand the sacrifice concept. More than ever, this generation strives to find the right balance between their personal lives and their business lives, and frankly, they are doing a much better job of it than did my baby boomer cohorts.

Now for the paradox: people accept that success in their lives requires some measure of personal sacrifice, but very few practice sacrifice within the workplace. Why not? Consider these possibilities:

1. Making business sacrifices is not part of their leadership or management DNA.
2. They have great difficulty sacrificing anything that has a deep personal and/or emotional attachment.
3. They do not believe that foregoing strategic initiatives and projects will improve business performance. The hard-core members of this clan go a step further—they think strategic sacrifice will only make things worse.

Let's look at each rationale. Firstly, there exists a sector of people who consciously choose not to make business-related sacrifices. An example would be leaders who dislike placing anything on the chopping block such as brands, processes, initiatives, and employees. To the contrary, they prefer more businesses, more brands, more line extensions, more stock keeping units, more inventories, more acquisitions, more of this, more of that. The paradigm within their psyche demands they do more, ideally with less (for efficiency and reduced costs), but sometimes with more (where revenue and margins supposedly outpace increased staffing expenses). This attitude creates business complexity and the management drawbacks that go with it. The healthier solution for the long haul is injecting strategic sacrifice into the complexity and focus standoff: *Complexity ÷ Sacrifice = Focus*. Yes, it looks easy. $E = mc2$ also looks easy. The trick is making the simple formula work.

Secondly, companies are stocked with individuals who understand the value of focus, but won't sacrifice anything to which there is a deep personal and/or emotional attachment. These people are not necessarily unsuccessful. Many pride themselves on getting others to do what they don't want to do—some bring in consultants to do their dirty work. Others delegate to capable subordinates. A good leader or manager convinces people they should want to make that call. Admirable leaders, however, get themselves to do what they (deep down) don't want to do. This can mean sacrificing sacred cows or drowning your puppies.

The third category is comprised of people who do not believe that strategic (and operational) sacrifice will improve business performance, but rather weaken it. As you now know from the first pages of this book, I was at this crossroad a long time ago. Having weathered that storm of product and brand rationalization, I never looked back. The experience of the difficult turnaround taught me that specialists will always beat generalists within their chosen fields. But sooner or later, C-suites, boards of directors, and investors shortchange the power of specialization and envision quick sales and earnings upsides from category proliferation—their theory being that fixed overheads are already in place, so newfound margin will drop to the bottom line. It will not. Coca-Cola, a beverage company, earns almost $9 billion on sales of $47 billion. By contrast, PepsiCo, a food and beverage company, exceeds its rival by 42 percent in turnover, but manages to deliver $1.8 billion less in earnings.

Several companies that were extremely successful operating in single market businesses such soda pop, soup, and cereal have chosen to become broad food companies to accelerate corporate growth. Wall Street likes top-line growth. They prefer seeing companies "do more and more" to get bigger and bigger, preferably with less and less—meaning fewer employees and lower operating costs. There is a cruel irony in this: those responsible for these moves have made a sacrifice, but they are blind to the sacrifice. Some forgo strategic focus and specialization to fast-track sales growth. Others look to the synergy advantages, but in case after case, profit-to-sales ratios decline. This happened to P&G when they entered the food business. P&G, believing that food manufacturing and marketing weren't that different from selling soap, gave food a good try, but they finally saw the light and exited, preferring the fat margins within categories such as beauty care where they could add value and get a better return.

Layering acquired businesses over existing fixed costs for enhanced margin is last-century thinking. Companies can realize a "synergy" savings, as Kraft did with the Jacobs Suchard acquisition, but eventually the strategic focus wanes and complexity creeps in. The fallacy in the logic is the "fixed costs." There is no such thing as fixed costs. Anything can be cut or sold, including bricks and mortar. Enhancing a company's strategic health should be the primary goal of an acquisition. Synergies are nothing more than a bonus.

Don't Let Fizz Become Fuzz

Former Coke CEO, Roberto Goizueta[2] knew plenty about sacrifice. His privileged life in Havana ended in 1960 when he was forced from Cuba by the Castro regime. With a few hundred dollars in his pocket, he worked his way to the top of Coca-Cola in America. You'd think his days of sacrifice would be over. Not so. Although Goizueta would never admit it, the now infamous New Coke was his ballistic missile that was developed to annihilate the embarrassing onslaught of his rival's taste test challenge. If you are a marketer, you know the rest of the story. New Coke became one of the greatest marketing blunders of all time.

That inference aside, take a moment to ponder the magnitude of this colossal gamble and misstep from a sacrificial point of view. When Goizueta became chief executive, he reportedly told his employees there would be no sacred cows at Coca-Cola. Most people would have viewed this edict as a tough-minded superlative. Hordes of newly appointed CEOs have made similar declarations in their initial salvos to the employee group. I'll venture a guess that no one in the Coca-Cola organization, other than perhaps Goizueta himself, believed this edict would apply to the company's time-honored cola recipe.

They were soon to find out that Goizueta was a man of his word. Somehow he overcame the trepidation of putting the company's crown jewels on the line. Goizueta killed Coca-Cola's darling. Seventy-nine days later, it was clear that the wheels had fallen off his streetcar named desire. That was the day that Goizueta reloaded his revolver and shot *his* puppy, New Coke. Coca-Cola Classic returned to the market, and the Coca-Cola Company returned to the fast lanes for good.

In his book, *Focus: The Future of Your Company Depends on It,* Al Ries states, "No two companies illustrate the power of a focus better than PepsiCo, Inc., and the Coca-Cola Company."[3] I read Al's book a long time ago, and although I was already a believer, I recall turning the pages as though it were a best-selling mystery novel. I reference this book to illustrate the longer-term benefits of strategic sacrifice. The Coca-Cola Company has made only one major venture outside of the beverage industry, and that was the purchase of Columbia Pictures 40 years ago. Goizueta turfed Columbia for an $800 million shareholder gain,[4] and after that transaction, the company never acquired anything that you could not drink. In *Focus*, Al Ries itemized the comparative values of Coke and Pepsi, using their 1994 and 1995 fiscal performances (see Table 1.1).

In the years to come, Coca-Cola would put corporate clarity, coherence, and specialization to good work. The company

Table 1.1 1994/95 Coca-Cola and PepsiCo Sales, Profit, and Market Value

1994/1995	*PepsiCo*	*Coca-Cola*	*Coke's Difference*	
Net Sales	$28.5 billion	$16.2 billion	−$12.3b	−43%
Net Income	$1.8	2.6	+$0.8	+44%
Market Value	$27.9	65.7	+$37.8	+135%

Table 1.2 2013 Coca-Cola and PepsiCo Sales, Profit, and Market Value

2013	*PepsiCo*	*Coca-Cola*	*Coke's Difference*	
Net Sales	$66.4 billion	$46.8 billion	−$19.6b	−30%
Net Income	$6.7	8.5	+1.8	+27%
Market Value*	$121.8	168.2	+46.4	+38%

Note: * February, 2014 Market Value

remains committed to beverages, and its performance 20 years later reinforces why specialists traditionally beat diversified generalists in the board game known as business (see Table 1.2).

Okay, so Pepsi has narrowed the gap, but at present, within the food and beverage industry, Coca-Cola is delivering an outstanding five-year profit-to-sales ratio of 22 percent,[5] despite a less-than-stellar 2013 performance. As for Pepsi, although it looked like the company was well on its way to trading the sparkle of fizz for the haze of fuzz, they recognized portfolio convolution and divested their underperforming restaurant businesses that included KFC, Pizza Hut, and Taco Bell in the late nineties. There are several ironies to this move, including the strategic reasoning found in PepsiCo's 1997 press release: "Our goal in taking these steps is to dramatically sharpen PepsiCo's focus," said Roger Enrico, the CEO at the time. If we take Enrico's statement at face value, he recognized the albatrosses he was carrying. Divesting those businesses would generate cash and free up management to do less, in order to do better in the soft drink and snacks business. Of course, if the restaurant businesses had been delivering acceptable earnings, the call might have been a very difficult sacrifice. One can only speculate on how long those earnings would continue before heading south.

The other irony is a personal one. Enrico's career path was every bit as interesting as that of his adversary, Goizueta. Unlike Goizueta, who came from a wealthy family, Enrico was the son of a small-town factory foreman. Shortly after he took the top job at PepsiCo, he said that you build a business by making big changes to big things. Enrico wasn't kidding. For two decades, PepsiCo has operated as a beverage and snack foods enterprise. With half of sales in food, PepsiCo, under the current leadership of its first female chief executive, Indra Nooyi, has delivered a five-year profit-to-sales ratio of 10 percent[6]—by no means shabby for any mega company engaged in the consumer packaged food business. Notwithstanding this accolade, the financials still favor Coke. Pepsi is 42 percent bigger in turnover, but worth 28 percent less in market cap and almost two billion less in earnings. Yep, category and strategic simplicity still go a long way.

The Tragic Fall from Specialist to Generalist

The vast majority of organizations begin as specialists. Some, like manufacturers of automobiles, fashion apparel, cosmetics, and pharmaceuticals, stay that way and continue to prosper. Others succumb to diversification and suffer the consequences of complexity and incoherence. Anheuser-Busch, Campbell's, ConAgra, and Hillshire Brands (formerly Sara Lee) are four companies that expanded into areas that challenged their core competencies and their ability to remain focused.

In the nineties, ConAgra was on a diversification spree that left them with several unrelated consumable categories, including prepared foods, snacks, and staples. Each category required a different management capability and a different set of success factors. In 2012, they purchased the frozen meals assets of Unilever for $265 million, and made a $5 billion bid to take over Ralcorp that closed in 2013. Ralcorp manufactures an assortment of foods, primarily private labels sold through consumer and foodservice channels.

If you aren't careful, the strategy of "get big at any cost" can spell disaster. The incoherence absurdity appears on the second page of ConAgra's 2012 Annual Report: "Our operating principles: simplicity, accountability, collaboration, innovation." As for the word "simplicity," I'm thinking this is either a typo or a failure by management to comprehend the meaning of the word. For the record, *Merriam-Webster's* dictionary defines simplicity as "the state of being uncomplicated or uncompounded."

It might surprise you that online retailer Amazon abides by that definition. Starting as an bookseller, Amazon now sells a vast collection of products, including music, DVDs, software, electronics, food, beauty aids, jewelry, sporting goods, apparel, baby products, and even scientific supplies. With that lineup, it would be easy to conclude that Amazon had lost their way and become a complex business. Not a chance. Amazon has not ventured beyond their core competency of online retailing. In fact, they have enhanced their superior logistics system and their customer service ethic to make the shopping experience one of the best within the online industry. In Amazon's case, it doesn't much matter what they sell; rather, it's how they sell it that counts. Core competencies can be around tangible items or processes. If a product line offers opportunity, fits the system and the core competency, and can live up to the Amazon promise, it's in the portfolio.

Anheuser-Busch (A-B) made the mistake of looking at the salty snacks market with the eye of a marketer, rather than the mind of a corporate strategist. Who couldn't argue that salty pretzels and peanuts go nicely with an ice cold beer? However, the marketers overlooked the fact that the scale of A-B's beer distribution system was the company's competitive advantage and key success factor. The way you ship cases of barley sandwiches isn't the way you ship cello or foil bags containing snacks and a lot of air. By 1996, A-B was done with Eagle Snacks, its five manufacturing facilities, and 1,750 employees.[7]

By the time I came on the scene to assist Interbrew (now Anheuser-Busch InBev) with a global brand positioning assignment, the world's five largest brewers were all sticking to their knitting. I met with Interbrew chief marketing officers (CMOs) from all over the world and never did we engage in discussions pertaining to anything other than beer. This consulting gig proved to be exceedingly refreshing. A-B has learned the lesson of category and core competency focus. ConAgra has not.

Sara Lee is synonymous with baking products. But to get bigger, faster, they added several unrelated businesses to their portfolio. Other than the fact that the ultimate purchaser may be the same, shoe polish, undergarments, and baked goods are as different as night and day. Sara Lee dumped Hanes in 2006, and in 2011, they found a better home for Kiwi in the house of SC Johnson, a well-defined company in the household cleaning products business.

Has Sara Lee learned their lesson? Renamed the Hillshire Brands Company, this conglomerate is engaged in a broad line of foods under more than a dozen brand names, including Jimmy Dean, Ball Park, Hillshire Farms, Chef Pierre, Bryan Foods, Van's, State Fair and oh, yeah...Sara Lee. In Hillshire's zeal to expand further, they went after Pinnacle Foods (Vlasic Pickles, Birds Eye, and Duncan Hines), and fell victim to an auction process that would see the entire company divested to Tyson Foods, netting shareholders an outrageous return of 70 percent more than Hillshire's market valuation before the bidding started.[8]

Twenty-five years ago, I had the pleasure of spending the better part of a day with Howard Schultz in Seattle. His product passion was Italian-style coffee, and his corporate goal was to create the best coffee company in the world through brand and product differentiation. Howard's success with Starbucks is an understatement. Two years ago, when Starbucks reported a desire to move away from its coffee "specialist" strategy, I feared his greatly diluted ownership in Starbucks no longer gave him the leverage to battle the whims of Wall Street. I figured Howard was yielding to stock market pressure to accelerate top-line growth. I loathed seeing Starbucks surrender "brand specificity" by adding a bunch of noncoffee-related products for the sake of bigness. At the time, I said this type of bigness was bad business. Surely, Starbucks would be better off backward integrating or adding products/services that would expand their world of coffee and fortify their premium coffee expertise imagery.

Notwithstanding this view, investors went on to reward Starbucks with an all-time high stock price 12 months later. Was this a matter of cause and effect? I think not. A promise to shift strategy from specialist to generalist does not create a 50 percent increase in shareholder value. The proof is in the economic pudding. Starbucks delivered an awesome top- and bottom line in 2013, verifying investor confidence, as well as the company's adeptness at continuing to grow profitably in coffee-related businesses. Their push in China has them at over a thousand stores in 60 cities.[9] If all goes according to plan, China will soon be Starbucks' second- largest market. Add to this a partnership with another roaster that facilitates a foray into single-serve coffee, plans to launch convenient single-serve coffee machines, and expansion into supermarkets, and you have this $15 billion company humming along within its niche. Even Wall Street can't argue with outstanding financial performance.

From a strategic standpoint, specialists enjoy so many more strategic attributes than do generalists. As seen in the Coke versus Pepsi scenario, specialists garner higher margins. I will never forget my initial shock at buying my first cup of Starbucks coffee. I paid for one cup what consumers were shelling out for half a pound of our ground supermarket coffee that would make 25 cups.

Secondly, specialists usually focus on one product, one benefit, and one message. In the fresh pizza category, it may look like everyone is a category specialist. However, even within one-category businesses, it is possible to see differences in positioning. In its early days, Domino's Pizza sacrificed a myriad of possible customer promises to concentrate on fresh and fast home delivery as their unique selling proposition. They were the first to guarantee 30-minute delivery. When competitive delivery systems improved, Domino's created a heat wave pad to make sure the pizza stayed hot. Of course, the entry chit in this business is great tasting pizza. No one wants bad pizza delivered fast. Along the way, the perception of Domino's quality began to suffer, so they embarked on a strategy to reboot it.

Despite the oversaturation of pizza-based outlets in America, the five-year trend in sales, profit, and market value indicates that Domino's product enhancement strategy is working. However, the delivery promise remains critical to success, and Domino's continues to work at maintaining this positioning advantage. Today, digital ordering is the name of the game. To make it faster and easier for customers to place and track orders, Domino's has made strategic investments in digital and mobile technology. Is it any wonder that about one-third of the company's 500 home-office employees work in the information technology (IT) department?[10]

By concentrating on one category only, the specialist should know that category better than multicategory competitors, a huge asset when it comes to running it.

Knee-deep in the Soup

Size and exceptional growth have their challenges. But in Starbucks' case, it has not created prolonged disruptive complexity. If you want to get the better of complexity and reap the rewards of doing less, better, I suggest the starting place is five basic questions:

1. Where is the complexity?
2. How did it rear its ugly head in the first place?
3. What should be done to reduce it?
4. Who can do it?
5. What should be sacrificed?

I'll address these questions using a former client as a case study. The Campbell Soup Company, with sales in over 120 countries, is the world's largest soup maker with a 60 percent market share in a $4 billion market.[11] Campbell's also competes in many other food categories. This company is very profitable—but there's a problem, a big problem. The Campbell Soup Company is stuck in the doldrums, struggling with several decades of stagnation within its core soup franchise. Making matters worse is a flat line on corporate sales and profits over the past five years.[12]

Q1: Where is the complexity? A1: Beginning as a soup specialist, Campbell's has become a food generalist. Initially operating a simple business of shelf stable products, the firm's tentacles have extended to an array of fresh, frozen, and refrigerated foods. I am talking about many businesses to digest, lead, and manage. It is one thing to market several products and brands within one form such as shelf stable, fresh, frozen, or refrigerated foods. It is quite another to engage in all four. This creates complexity, from inbound logistics and operations all the way to outbound logistics and sales and service. Principle number one: the less coherent the businesses, the greater the complexity throughout the value chain.

Q2: How did complexity rear its ugly head in the first place? A2: Since 1980, under the watch of five CEOs, Campbell's has failed to ignite its highly profitable US soup franchise. Over those years, these CEOs have purchased and rearranged several chairs on a broadening deck of businesses and brands. I suspect there was serious doubt as to whether stimulating US soup sales would be adequate to satisfy shareholder thirsts, and as such, generations of top brass have succumbed to the "purported" safety net of diversification.

Q3: What should be done to reduce the complexity? A3: When the company spun off some businesses such as Vlasic Pickles and Swanson's frozen dinners, it said it would focus on four core areas; soups, sauces and beverages, biscuits and confectionery, and foodservice. Even those four (I count six) core areas sounded like they could use some focus. In my consultancy capacity, I tried to shake up the folks at Campbell's with a transformational agenda designed to bend their problematic soup trend. One of my recommendations was a page from the Starbucks book—a model I'd come to understand and appreciate. I recommended they consider launching high-end fresh soup bistros in America's major urban markets. Who better to do this than America's renowned soup maker? Who better to showcase soup expertise and enhance the image of a legendary soup expert? To me, the concept, from the house of Campbell's, offered tremendous domestic and global growth opportunities.

But when I presented the idea, the fellow who presided over the US soup division looked at me like I was nuts. "We aren't in the restaurant business," he said. "Our mandate is to figure out how to bolster sales of condensed soup." By this time, I'd already concluded that his mandate was trying to hang on to his job. He'd do that by impressing his boss with slick presentations on the "big picture" opportunities for condensed soup, thereby demonstrating his competence as a divisional president.

As for my mandate, I responded with, "Why not get our feet wet with a couple of bistro tests?" No, not even that was going to fly. A big bushy tree blocked his view of a lush forest. More than a decade later, you can walk the streets of New York City and find dozens of terrific soup restaurants. One chain, Hale & Hearty, operates 29 outlets in Manhattan alone. You'd think by now, someone at Campbell's might have given soup bistros a "hearty" try. Not so. When you grow via acquisition, you soon forget how to grow organically.

Q4: Who can cut through the complexity? A4: The responsibility rests with the CEO and the Board. But there must be a *will* before there is a *way*. Campbell's leaders either stopped thinking like a soup specialist or never thought like one in the first place. They yielded to the lure of acquisition to expand the categories in which they compete—now, they have to run them. In the meantime, their soup stagnation continues—but not everyone else's.

General Mill's Progresso brand has been growing for ten years and hovers at 40 percent of the ready-to-serve market. Small players are growing even faster. In 2012, soup sales of companies with niche positioning such as Pacific Soups and Amy's Kitchen Soups grew by 10 percent. If those companies can figure out how to expand soup, why can't Campbell's? The issue isn't money; it's mind-set.

Has anything changed under Campbell's current regime? Recent acquisitions of Bolthouse Farms juices, Plum Organics, and Kelsen Group (baked goods) tell me they're digging themselves in deeper. This 2012 and 2013 expansion added a couple of hundred items of fresh, shelf stable, frozen, and refrigerated beverages, dressings, snacks, and baby foods. Several recalls from shorter shelf lives are but one indication of increased complexity. This isn't the stuff that's going to free up management hours to deal with soup's sluggishness in the home market. Nor are new soup entries in stand-up pouches and dinner sauces in black packages going to conjure up images of café blackboards. Those cafés could have, and should have, been Campbell's soup bistros. Despite annual report website rhetoric about "reshaping the portfolio for the future" and "leveraging breakthrough innovation," this company continues to operate under the "do more of the same, but better" strategy.

Q5: What should be sacrificed? A5: Condensed soup is a sacred cow because of its extraordinary profit contribution. Consumers couldn't care less. They prefer the more convenient ready-to-serve offerings such as the Chunky subbrand. This raises the issue of cannibalization of condensed, and that is blasphemy in the Campbell's offices at Camden, New Jersey. I'm guessing that none of the CEOs were prepared to put their necks on the line by declaring the condensed soup business a dead duck in this time-starved consumer era of convenience and mobility. Fifty years ago, Campbell's condensed canned soup was the staple of America's Main Street. Today, there is no Main Street. For the record, my recommendation was not to kill the darling, but to milk it and aggressively push ready-to-serve soups everywhere, not fretting about cannibalization. Oh, yes, it would be remiss of me not to make you aware of a second sacrifice—Wall Street would have to accept some short-term pain, and as you know, Wall Street isn't very good at sacrifice.

Consider how Goizueta or Enrico might have dealt with the situation. From what I have read of these leaders, they were changemakers prepared to make sacrifices in return for the rewards of the big play. Sure, Goizueta took a huge gamble with New Coke, but he also rose from the ashes to save the day. Enrico, often credited with the Pepsi Challenge, was the guy who killed his advertising darling and replaced it with "The Choice of a New Generation," a blockbuster campaign launched by Michael Jackson to the beat and melody of "Billy Jean."

Earlier in the chapter, I stated three reasons why business people fail to practice the tenets of sacrifice and focus. Reason number three applies to the Campbell Soup Company—their leaders (and Wall Street) do not believe that strategic sacrifice will improve corporate performance. Another way to put it is to say, they don't have the confidence in their ability to do it.

Prune What You Plant

Good gardeners know that pruning is as important as planting. Good companies make a habit of taking stock of their crop. This can sidestep the urgency of savage asset and employment pruning when things turn sour. Pruning should be as perpetual as the daily rising of the sun, and it isn't limited to senior management. People at all levels of the organization can partake in pruning every day of the week. Don't tell me that you need all those reports that appear on your computer screen every morning, or the printed copies that pile up on the corner of your desk. Finance and IT love to produce reports in the hope that you will put the data to good use.

Truth be known, the finance department is often overlooked as a ruthless pruning agent because the big cuts usually come from the top. But as an ongoing strategy to do less, better, the astute financial manager or chief financial officer (CFO) laboriously asks *whether* and *how* reports are being used, and who is on the distribution list. If the CFO doesn't like the answers, the pruning shears come out and some darlings may be killed. To facilitate this culture, finance departments must elevate themselves beyond nitpicking about costs. Without foregoing finance and administration best practices, they must address the complexity conundrums that arise within systems and procedures that are ineffective, inefficient, and arduous.

Big data is not going away. Its flood of details about trends and behaviors of customers, competitors, markets, and employees has become part of the everyday practice for everybody. According to the McKinsey Global Institute, "big data will become a key basis of competition, underpinning new waves of productivity growth, innovation, and consumer surplus." McKinsey seems to think leaders in every sector will have to grapple with the implications of big data, and that various factors will fuel exponential growth in data for the foreseeable future.[13] That sounds like a complexity risk. Of course, one must be mindful that complexity for one company can be the advantage for a nimble and focused competitor.

I'm suggesting that 80 percent of the data in a person's inbox either never gets opened or seldom gets a glance. This brings me to Pareto's Principle, the 80/20 rule, occasionally known as the law of the vital few. The principle is more than a century old, and is rooted in Vilfredo Pareto's simple observation that 20 percent of the pea pods in his garden contained 80 percent of the peas. This led to a more profound assertion by Pareto—that 80 percent of the land in Italy was owned by 20 percent of the population.[14] You've likely heard this expression in business as it applies to sales, profits, and customers. I found the principle extremely helpful in identifying the projects and initiatives in which to invest time and money. Generally speaking, 20 percent of the new initiatives deliver 80 percent of the rewards. Choose carefully, and you save money, reduce complexity, and ride the fastest racehorses to the future.

Before leaving this chapter, I want to pose a final question: would you expect to see layers of complexity in a company with sales of $469 billion, 11,000 locations, and hundreds of thousand stock keeping units? Based on what you've read so far about specialists and generalists, you might be persuaded to say "yes." Think again. This giant is Walmart, the world's largest and most respected retailer. Walmart knows how to simplify.

They operate in 27 countries and employ 2.2 million people—there are 90 countries on the globe with populations under 2.2 million. The executives of the world's largest and most successful retailer aren't fussed by their company's size or scope. Every country management team is clear on the two or three things that make their Walmart tick.

Although barely into the book, I've trumpeted specialization as a winning business strategy. To give my premise traction, I have used unfocused "generalists" as the foil. Do not assume that every generalist strategy is a recipe for disaster or that big is always bad. There are hordes of great companies that success-fully sell soup to nuts without carrying the weight of a complex-ity albatross on their shoulders.

The secret to Walmart's success is an IT infrastructure that facilitates the rituals of a superior logistics and supply man-agement system. By accurately forecasting demand, tracking and predicting inventory levels, creating efficient transporta-tion routes, and managing customer relationships and service response logistics, Walmart enjoys the highest sales per square foot, enviable inventory turnover, and the best profit of any retailer.[15]

P&G is a good gardener. For almost 180 years, it has been pruning, organically planting, and buying new gardens in which to nourish. Although they plant more than they prune as measured by sales value, P&G have lopped off some sizable divisions, including the prescription drug business, and the food division, which included Folgers, Jif, Crisco and Pringles. More recently, a deal with Mars for $2.9 billion in 2014 will see the divestiture of Iams and Eukanuba—P&G realizes that they can't invest their time and money in everything. They choose to invest in the brands and markets that will offer higher returns, and rid themselves of the rest. Beyond this pruning, P&G has killed several darlings from their esteemed past. Here are just 7 of 80 brands that they have either sold or terminated[16] (see table 1.3).

Table 1.3   7 Time-Honored P&G Darlings Killed or Sold

Brand	Created	Killed
Ivory Flakes	1910	1977 (discontinued)
Oxydol	1914	2000 (sold to Redox Brands)
Noxema	1914	2008 (sold to Alberto-Culver)
Spic and Span	1933	2001 (sold to Shansby Group)
Clearasil	1940	2000 (sold to Boots Group)
Duncan Hines	1952	1997 (sold to Aurora Foods)
Comet	1956	2001 (sold to Prestige Brands)

P&G is currently organized into four global units predicated on the commonality of consumer benefits, technologies, and competitors.

Chapter 1 Summary

- Complexity alienates customers, contaminates cultures, heightens stress, and increases the cost of doing business.
- When business complexity increases, managerial complexity isn't far behind. When managerial complexity increases, business complexity isn't far behind.
- Stamping out complexity won't happen without a strong will to change.
- Along with the *will*, you must be rationally and emotionally convinced that focus through sacrifice will take you to a better place. That is the *why* and the *how*.
- The sacrifices that affect you personally require courage.
- In the land of the blind, the one-eyed man is King. All you have to do is make sure that you are better than your chosen competitor, and that you improve quicker than they do.
- Specialists beat generalists, but generalists who embrace and practice focus can be wildly successful.
- Like gardening, pruning is as important as planting in business. Plant, prune, and prosper.

CHAPTER 2

The Steel and Steal of Strategic Sacrifice

"Strategy" has to be the most misunderstood and misused word in business. The word is tossed around boardrooms, water coolers, and customer meetings with reckless abandon. At the risk of sounding elementary, I have to reiterate at a very basic but consequential level, that strategy occurs away from the day-to-day action. It is the big picture. Deciding to become a global corporation, to enter new markets, or to increase sales by a million widgets per annum is not strategy.

You've likely heard people say, "Our strategy is to become the biggest and the best." Such aspirations are goals or objectives. Strategy is not the *what*, but the *how*—how you will become the biggest and the best is strategy's raison d'être, its reason for being. Of course, the strategy you choose to achieve that goal can be good or bad. The *steel* in strategy is its capacity to set the stage for organizations to achieve ironclad competitive advantages. Ironclad is a strong word, but it doesn't necessarily imply sustainability. Some of the steel that flows from your strategy may not stand the test of time. All it really has to do is ensure that your advantages are better than those of your competition. That's not to say that you shouldn't seek sustainable competitive advantage. Lofty goals have a way of delivering lofty results.

Beyond the *steel* of strategy is the *steal* that strategy affords. Strategy is a steal because good strategies cost no more to develop than bad ones. Sound simple enough? Not so fast. There's a host of leaders out there who understand the definition of strategy and its virtues, but continue to struggle with their own strategies and implementations.

This profound assertion comes from the Strategy & (formerly Booz & Company) 2013 survey of 3,500 global leaders that included 550 CEOs and 325 other C-suite executives. The report cites lack of cohesion within the organization as the reason for most managers' failing to understand the company's strategy. Consider these statistics: 54% of respondents didn't believe their company's strategy would lead to success, and 53% couldn't say whether their employees even understood the strategy. Only a third believed their company's core capabilities fully supported the corporate strategy.[1] Ouch!

A clear strategic course begins the process of coherence, and once everyone is on board, wise leaders shouldn't deviate. Ponder for a moment, strategy's four fundamental questions:

1. What business are you in?
2. What will you sell?
3. To whom will you sell?
4. How will you sell?

These questions have been around for a long time, but they still work. I have posed them to hundreds of executives and brand managers. You would think I'd get reasonably similar responses from members of the same management team. But think again. People struggle with specificity because they abhor strategic confinement. Even though most senior executives know that being all things to all people is a blueprint for disaster, they can't help themselves. They cannot ignore the lure and their lust for opportunity—any opportunity to increase sales. Their logic is this: more balls in the air present more chances of success. However, the reverse is actually true. More balls in the air divert attention, muddle direction, increase complexity, and in the long run, add to the risk of failure.

Some of these folks choose poor strategies because of their ambiguity. Others mistake tactics for strategy. Tactics are the short-term decisions and activities that win battles and help win wars. Sales departments know tactics better than most other functions because salespeople work with tactics all the time. Every day of the week, retail-merchandising managers contemplate this question: what products and brands will we promote in our bargain sale, and at what price? Retailers can't answer that question without a firm understanding of daily, weekly, and monthly tactics. To thrive in the retail business, a model that can be awfully complex, the best retailers focus on the few key success factors that deliver the goods.

Promoting Tide Detergent as a loss leader or trying to make a small or large profit margin on the brand is a tactic. If the retailer's market positioning is the "lowest sale price" for brand name items, then all pricing tactics must support that image. In this example, because of Tide's broad consumer appeal, a healthy margin that inflates the price of the product would be unwise because selling Tide at a price above competition doesn't fit the retailer's positioning. Imagine the customer ramifications if Walmart, with a "low prices every day" reputation, did that. Conversely, a "lowest sale price" retailer doesn't have to lose money selling Tide. Their options are either to squeeze the makers of Tide into lowering their cost for a period of time, or choosing another brand with similar consumer appeal from another supplier. That's tactical decision-making.

Walmart has long envied the online business of Amazon.com. In the years that Amazon was driving sales by expanding product lines and customer count, Walmart was doing a nice job of opening new outlets and increasing same-store sales. But now, like so many other brick-and-mortar retailers, Walmart is playing catch-up with its concerted effort into digital commerce. This is an objective. Walmart's strategy, their means to that end, is a growing web presence, an array of mobile apps, and an infrastructure designed and operated by the best managers, coders, and engineers the digital world has to offer. These folks can be found in a large and growing outpost called WalmartLabs in the Bay Area at San Bruno. Walmart.com's competitive advantage in digital, according to Senior Vice-President Gibu Thomas, is that Walmart is not only bringing the store to the web, but it is bringing the web to the store through mobile.[2] The goal is to create a seamless shopping experience for Walmart's shoppers, who see their mobiles as an excellent resource for researching and buying the rapidly increasing number of online items.

I don't know enough about digital retailing to say whether there is steel in a strategy that comes off as generic. Superficially, the strategy doesn't differentiate from other brick-and-mortar retailers. But when you consider that Walmart is the biggest, the most efficient, and the lowest cost retailer, clout comes into play. With online sales of $10 billion and a growth rate of 30 percent for the 2013/14 fiscal, Walmart.com is already the fourth-largest online retailer, trailing only Amazon, Apple, and Staples.[3] Who better to leverage their massive customer base and reap the rewards of the expanding digital world of retailing?

In my CEO afterlife, I view such matters with greater clarity from a far less muddled place. I'm not backing off my passionate belief in the value of strategy in business—strategy is in my DNA, and partnered with the creative mind-set, this duo has proven itself to be an awesome armory throughout my career. The truth of the matter is that strategy and creativity without tactics aren't worth much. Without tactics, a corporation's performance and shareholder value are greatly diminished.

Why Mission Statements Suck

The vision of the game should be a clear definition of where a company is going and what sets it apart from the rest of the pack. In so many corporations, the mission statement that comes from hours of navel-gazing fails to fulfill these critical objectives. My beef is the way in which guiding principles are crafted and communicated. So many mission statements are character-ized by verbose, convoluted arrangements of platitudes incapa-ble of resonating with employees. If you can't connect with your workforce, you sure as hell can't inspire them. I'm not the first and I'll surely not be the last to take issue with the vision/mis-sion statements that hang in lobbies and corporate boardrooms. Companies large and small, from newbies to blue chippers, con-tinue to err in shaping meaningful mantras.

Here's what the Exxon Mobil Corporation had to say about who they are and what they do: "We are committed to being the world's premier petroleum and petrochemical company. To that end, we must continuously achieve superior financial and oper-ating results while adhering to the highest standards of business conduct. These unwavering expectations provide the founda-tion for our commitments to those with whom we interact."[4] How many of their 82,000 employees will embrace or remember something like that? Exxon Mobil might just as well have said, "We want to make heaps of cash, honestly." My version is likely true, but it sure isn't motivating.

Then there is Staples, a $25 billion business that delivered a steady 5 percent return on revenue until a disastrous 2013 when they fell into the red. I suggest to you that Staples' mission statement serves little purpose other than making the manage-ment feel warm and fuzzy. Someone in power at Staples seems to think the words "soulful" and "holistic" can work for a store in the office supply business. I think they are kidding themselves. What about you? Are your emotions roused by these introductory sentences of their mission statement? "Staples Soul reflects our commitment to corporate responsibility. It's a holistic approach to business that recognizes the close connection between our financial success and our desire to make a positive impact on our associates, communities, and the planet by joining together the following areas: diversity, the environment, our community, and ethics. It is how we do business—that's Staples Soul."[5] This is only the preamble. Another 180 words of fluff on diversity, environment, community, and ethics is still to come—not one mention of the product, the service, or the customer.

I'm a fan of the Panera Bread chain. When I lived in Ventura, California, this was one of my favorite lunch stops. I liked Panera's ambiance, their speed of service, their hospitality, and their variety of offerings. "A loaf of bread in every arm" is Panera Bread's mission. I suspect its development was guided by the desire to communicate the organization's specialty. This statement is as simple as a mission statement gets, but what does it mean and what does it achieve? Does "a loaf of bread in every arm" guide or motivate employees in their daily duties, interactions, and decision-making?

Because the Panera employees who have assisted me have been exemplary, I can only assume that the motivation and direction that inspires these front-line workers comes from a team of capable regional or zone leaders. That weighty value is good enough to trump the message in any mission statement.

"Brothers First, Business Second" is one of the best mission statements I have ever seen. The caption happens to be handwritten on a faded framed wall photo of two youngsters who look to be six or seven years old. The photo used to hang on the wall of an Italian eatery owned and operated by the middle-aged brothers. When I saw it for the first time, I was struck by positive emotion. Having never met either of the brothers, I knew that I'd like them. Furthermore, that sentiment instantly impacted my presumption about the quality of the food they would serve. Deliver the goods, and they had a customer for life.

Howard Schultz grew Starbucks at an extraordinary pace. In three decades, Starbucks catapulted from America's Pacific Northwest to 61 countries. Howard's vision for Starbucks was a social community with a defined culture that people would aspire to connect with (over a cup of distinctive, dark-roasted coffee). Seemingly, the personality of the brand impacted every decision relating to the experience and the ambiance—the furniture, the artwork, the exotic names of the bean origins, and even the in-store music. "2000 by 2000" was all Starbucks' needed to say 20 years ago. Howard wanted 2,000 stores up and running by the new millennium. In his mind, rapidly establishing new stores in ideal locations was the most important thing Starbucks could do in the nineties. Starbucks achieved the target two years ahead of plan. That did not happen without every employee's involvement in expanding and operating the new locations, as well as working together to support their leader's clearly defined purpose.

Walmart's mission statement and advertising slogan have been the same for some time. I've always liked "Saving People Money So They Can Live Better," and its shorter version, "Save Money. Live Better." When you think of Walmart's ability to deliver, the claim makes good sense. But slogans tend to change faster than missions. I have also seen the tagline, "Low Prices Every day On Everything." This may be a better sales pitch, but does it offer a better purpose to Walmart's 2.2 million employees? I think not.

A worthwhile trick to writing mission statements is limiting the statement to no more than ten words. If you do that, you will have made the tough decision in describing the company's true premise. Strategic sacrifice brings clarity and focus. Simple, emotionally meaningful missions bring results.

Can You See the Forest for the Trees?

My affection for strategy might have something to do with the fact that I can be stubborn. Good strategists are also stubborn. They have to be. If you aren't strategically stubborn, you will allow the hard barrier lines that contain your strategy to blur. This jeopardizes a company's specificity and hinders the *do less, better* mode of operation. Despite the need for precision in purpose and direction, I see more and more examples of senior people operating nonstrategically. We used to call this "doing business by the seat of the pants." Like chickens running around with their heads chopped off, these busy, misdirected leaders either don't understand strategy, believe strategy is a deterrent to opportunity, or have never experienced the strategic disciplines of a prudent mentor. Truth is, they have never realized nor enjoyed the sales and profit rewards that come from walking away from nonstrategic ventures in the name of maintaining the integrity of strategic focus. Strategy is critical to clarity.

The irony of strategy is the fact that the best strategies require sacrifice. Strategy tells you what not to do. Once strategists carve out their course of action, the wisest of the owls stick to it like crazy glue. They don't want to hear about the infinite, untapped opportunities at the top of Mount Elsewhere. They want to know how to best trek Mount Here, the vista everyone on the expedition agreed to climb in the first place. At the top of Mount Here is the pot of gold.

Years ago I had the displeasure of counseling a large natural gas company in British Columbia. They wanted some help with marketing strategy. For me to do my job, I needed to ensure that we were all on the same page from 30,000 feet. This rocky road began with a strategy seminar to define the company's key success factors. Early in the seminar, I posed those four basic strategic questions to the management group. I expected "what business are you in?" to be a no-brainer. I was in for a shock.

The divisional general manager told me they were in the peace-of-mind business. At first blush, his answer aroused my senses, but on reflection, it was ambiguous. If this gas company were in the peace-of-mind business, the competition would range from insurance companies to couriers.

Amazon is arguably one of tech's most strategic companies. Venkatesh Rao, a *Forbes* contributor, summed it up quite nicely. "The entire company operates with what you might call a game mind," he said. "Not a product-building mind, not a marketing mind, not a sales mind. The key to a great game mind is having a preternatural ability to figure out which game to play, against which opponent. And once you've decided what game you're in, aligning the entire company so that it has the capacity to play that specific game better than anybody else. Half of Amazon's victories are won before the game even begins, because Amazon is so good at picking the right game and committing whole-heartedly to becoming really good at it."[6] Amen.

Jeff Bezos referred to strategic vision this way: "Any time you do something big, that's disruptive—Kindle, AWS (Amazon Web Services)—there will be critics. And there will be at least two kinds of critics. There will be well-meaning critics who genuinely misunderstand what you are doing or genuinely have a different opinion. And there will be the self-interested crit-ics that have a vested interest in not liking what you are doing and they will have reason to misunderstand. And you have to be willing to ignore both types of critics. You listen to them, because you want to see, always testing, is it possible they are right? But if you hold back and you say, 'No, we believe in this vision,' then you just stay heads down, stay focused and you build out your vision."[7] This is the mind of a strategist.

Strategy should never slow a company down or limit its growth opportunities. Specificity doesn't mean strategic blindness. Where there is an innovative way to create new market space, utilize core competencies, and enhance a brand's core image, go for it. Big companies can be fast and innovative if they sac-rifice those "opportunities" that lead to corporate incoherence. Leaders who say "no" to hundreds of "new and exciting" projects understand that vitality comes from focusing on the few that are truly meaningful and consistent with the company's core com-petencies and purpose.

When Larry Page became Google CEO in 2011, he made some organizational moves that let everyone know that Google was going to revitalize the commercialization of its innovations. Success in the future would not come from bottom-up innovation originated by the engineers who worked one day a week on their own projects and ideas. Page instituted a focused top-down approach in which senior members of the leadership team were charged with specific product/market accountabilities— seven groups in all, including video, advertising, search, operating systems, and apps. Gone from the mix was a laundry list of products and applications that were either integrated into other products or shot. Page's disdain for complexity and bureaucracy was central to the transformation.

Swiss-based Nestlé is the largest food manufacturing company in the world. Nestlé is also extremely strategic. They made the choice to enter the single-serve coffee and coffee machine business. They had good reason. For decades, the only convenient method for making a single cup of coffee came from a jar of instant coffee. The taste was unpleasant, but Nestlé, with the Nescafé brand, was the global leader in this declining category. Nescafé is coffee, and Nespresso is a brilliant extension of the mother ship's brand positioning. This is innovation at its best. Nespresso doesn't take Nestlé outside of its core competence or its strategic positioning; this breakthrough enhances it.

It took Nestlé a long time to pioneer and succeed with the Nespresso concept, but they persisted, and today Nespresso products deliver turnover of $5 billion at double-digit growth rates.[8] The sales of single-serve brewing machines (the hardware) and single-serve packets and pods (the software) delivered approximately $35 billion and $8 billion respectively in 2013. That's more than a mug of beans for two markets that didn't exist 25 years ago. It's no wonder Starbucks, via acquisition, is the latest major brand entry in this category. With these volume and growth characteristics, consumers can expect lower price entries and private label brands to take a swig of this lucrative category.

Sticking to strategy in the good times of vibrant markets and healthy margins is easy. The moment there is a downturn in the economy or a couple of bad quarters of profitability, however, leaders blink. Panic sets in. Costs are cut, and the strategic agenda takes a backseat. This method of operation does not advance a company's strategic health.

Porsche is currently enjoying a vibrant auto market. One of the reasons for their success is their decision to distinguish themselves by the fact that every vehicle is made in Germany. The German-made differentiator affords a high-quality image, and for that, Porsche enjoys significantly higher prices per vehicle and a higher operating margin ratio than does Mercedes-Benz, which now produces and/or assembles a wide range of autos in more than 25 countries. Mercedes' decision to position themselves as an affordable choice to a broader socioeconomic target group is quickly moving them into the generalist category of auto manufacturing. A Mercedes-Benz is no longer a car just for the wealthy. Lower production costs have made that possible.

Porsche should be delighted by this. The proud and differentiated "Made in Germany" brand claim is stronger, and Porsche's specialty lineup and narrow target group facilitates super premium pricing. But now, under Volkswagen ownership, it seems that Porsche has also succumbed to the profit opportunity afforded by lower, nondomestic labor costs. In 2016, the Cayenne will be produced in Slovakia. According to Matthias Müller, Porsche CEO, all production locations will have to achieve the same high standards.[9] Sure, Matthias. We heard that from Mercedes-Benz when they moved production away from Germany.

Is there a Porsche customer out there who thinks that "Made in Slovakia" will improve brand value? This is nothing more than a case of cutting costs without regard for the value of the Porsche brand and the power of "German-made" in enhancing image, and correspondingly, enhancing prices. I'm betting that the Cayenne is just the tip of the iceberg.

Why Big *and* Small Companies Should Do Less, Better

Management guru Peter Drucker was the first to state the strategic difference between "doing things right" and "doing right things." Most boards and C-suite executives want their companies to do things right. For all intents and purposes, this is the substantiation of a well-managed organization. Doing things right concerns itself with management; doing right things is about leadership. Said another way, doing things right is operational, while doing right things is strategic. Strategic leadership is the window to strategic change, the forerunner to strategic advantage.

Companies have plenty of generic strategic choices at their disposal. But you don't have to be a specialist to achieve the rewards of clarity, simplicity, and focus. Jacobs Suchard thrived in just two product categories, chocolate and coffee. As for the business I headed from Vancouver, that specialist posture was personified by our premium brands, Toblerone, Milka, Côte d'Or, Nabob, and Swiss Water decaffeinated coffee. The acquisition by Kraft Foods abruptly ended the specialty market mind-set. I should know. I worked under the acquirer for the better part of a year. Inherent in Kraft's mass market mind-set is a culture of *doing more with less*. They acquire companies at a frantic rate and then enact synergies to bolster the bottom line, accelerate the payout of the acquisition, and go forward with even better scale economies than before. I call this the "quantitative" strategy. If you have deep pockets, buying a company and cutting the overheads isn't that difficult to do. Wall Street couldn't be happier with those companies that do this well.

When an organization enjoys "big company" power, a "qualitative" strategy isn't nearly as urgent. "Qualitative" strategies are about such factors as the creativity, the ingenuity, and the innovation created by the human resource versus the financial resource. At a recent investor conference, Barry Calpino, a Kraft Foods executive with the title of vice-president for breakthrough innovation, said the company was "early in the journey" of innovation and that Kraft's record had not been strong. "A big part of becoming really good at innovation has been facing the brutal facts and getting better," he said. "We were worst at innovation by almost any measure, qualitative, quantitative, outsider, insider, any way we looked at it. We benchmarked ourselves near our peer set in 2008 and we were near the bottom. Nearly everything we launched was considered a failure."[10] Obviously, Calpino is keen to change that. His job won't be easy. The power that comes with bigness has a way of deflating urgency and accountability for innovation.

To round out Kraft's view on innovation, let's take a peek at the big sister, Mondelez. Mondelez believes their global chocolate future is in the hands of "4 power brands, three priority markets, and two innovation platforms." The two innovation platforms are described as "bite size" and "bubbly." Bubbly is aerated chocolate similar to Nestlé's Aero brand chocolate bar, launched in 1935. In a speech to attendees of Barclays Back to School Conference, Bharat Puri, Mondelez senior vice-president and leader of the chocolate division, said, "Our bubbly platform has invigorated aerated tablets with its playful molded design."[11] Compare this view of innovation to Nestlé's single-serve coffee concept or Red Bull's event marketing breakthroughs.

For companies short on clout, the trick to sustainable competitive advantage is a culture of entrepreneurial and innovative thinking. Make the right move, shatter market paradigms, and your competitors have to follow. And while they are scrambling to catch up, you can be working on the next move to once again alter the strategic game. That culture emanates from the top and permeates every nook and cranny of the operation. The leader cannot do it alone. He or she needs other leaders, and they are everywhere, waiting to be unleashed.

Make no mistake. When a risk-averse CEO is hired or promoted into the corner office, the entrepreneurial spirit that once drove the enterprise can dissipate in days. Conversely, a new boss charged with unraveling a morose bureaucracy and transforming it into nimbleness must shift the mentality of the entire organization. No matter how hard he or she tries, some people refuse to change. By the end of those "turnaround" years at Jacobs Suchard in Canada, we were firmly entrenched in a *do right things* state of mind. People who weren't focused, passionate, creative, and competitive didn't do well within that organization. In fact, a director of a competitor's board once referred to us as a gang. This description was the supreme compliment, and we marched forward to strengthening our gang along the way with superb talents of like-mind.

In those tough turnaround days, success wasn't enough. The other guy had to fail. Over the years, I've learned that this isn't necessarily the way to succeed in business. That frame of mind worked for us when the bank was at our front step waiting for payment. But after all those sacrifices, *doing less better*, and restoring profitability and strategic health, I grew to realize that it was senseless to engage in bitter wars that challenged the profit margins of a burgeoning market. A rival doesn't have to fail; they too, can make a profit. But they cannot be permitted to lead; they must play catch-up.

Snails and Giants

If big organizations were animals, they'd be snails because they move at a snail's pace. Every day, I either hear or read about situations that roll along in bureaucracy—government is the biggest offender. But anyone who has worked with large non-government, not-for-profit organizations (NGOs) or giant corporations has tasted the escargot. Yes, there are exceptions. The most valuable tech businesses on the planet have set a wonderful example for getting things done. But unlike Apple and Google, most big companies don't have the will or the way to cut through the quagmire of red tape that negates expediency. Even 175+ year-old P&G, a company I greatly admire, struggles to find nimbleness.

While the speed of a snail may best represent bureaucracies, there are several more similarities shared by the species. Were you aware that snails are deaf? So are the leaders of some of the largest companies in America. I'd suggest hearing aids for the executives of AT&T, Bank of America, the four biggest airlines, and several cable operators, including Charter Communications and Time Warner.[12] Consumers aren't shy about telling these companies what they want and why they are dissatisfied with the services these giants provide. If the leaders of these companies can hear, why aren't they listening? Is it because they, like snails, live in protective shells?

The shell that encompasses big companies is not brick and mortar; it is clout and cash. Inside a snail's shell is a cold and dark environment that I suspect is similar to the one Monsanto inhabits. Despite a preponderance of concern over this company's genetically modified organism (GMO) practices, Monsanto doesn't deviate from its unwavering purpose of domination. Clout is their strategy. But this strategy is often overlooked or concealed, especially by the very organizations that thrive because of the power of clout.

Kraft/Mondelez strengthened their clout through acquisition (General Foods was the first big catch, then came Tombstone Pizza, Nabisco, Jacobs Suchard, Danone Biscuits, and Cadbury). But to hear Kraft/Mondelez tell it, the company's phenomenal growth is the result of astute brand building. Yes, there is truth to this, but for the record, the brand building they refer to was not their doing. This good work was performed by the brand builders of the acquired companies. Nonetheless, sheer size provides huge economies of scale throughout their operation, especially in production, overheads, distribution, and marketing. The consequence is a tremendous competitive edge in the marketplace.

Seldom will you hear about clout from the leaders of successful behemoths. More likely, you will hear about "unleashing the power of people, leveraging iconic brands, creating performance-driven values-led organizations, transforming markets, driving efficiency to fuel growth, and protecting the well-being of the planet."[13] Don't for a minute believe that the most important element responsible for Kraft's top-tier profit returns will be deflated with the split into two companies. The new Mondelez boasted sales of $35 billion in 2013, and the business that remains Kraft generated $18 billion. $18 billion is still a hell of a lot of cheese slices, bowls of peanuts, and cups of coffee.

In the petroleum industry where access to oil is tight, Exxon Mobil and Royal Dutch Shell say they are adjusting their strategies to meet the growing demand for alternative energies. You might think the current squeeze on oil supply would hurt their bottom lines. Yet although 2013 profits were down, the five-year profitability of both companies is exceedingly lucrative.

Exxon Mobil, with refineries 50 percent larger than the industry average, is one of the few giants prepared to declare the superior scale of their refineries as a formidable competitive advantage. I salute them for their honesty. Shell stays clear of clout, choosing to articulate a broad spectrum of competitive strategies, including improved efficiencies, the strength of the Shell brand, global exploration, and focused acquisitions.

Here's the point. When you know you will never be the low-cost producer nor will you ever have enough cash to outspend the big cat, you have no choice but to find other ways to skin it. There is absolutely no reason why a smaller player cannot challenge a giant's wallop and become a leader within its chosen market. The trick to thriving against the giants comes down to *doing less, better* with an arsenal of three weapons—strategy, creativity, and culture. Here are eight traits that help smaller players survive in a corporate world in which big keeps getting bigger:

1. The big guys are slow. Hustle.
2. They are bureaucratic. Be nimble.
3. They are risk averse. Think entrepreneurially.
4. They are generalists. Be a specialist or organize the company to act like one.
5. They value "doing things right." Prioritize "doing right things."
6. They are obsessed with scale. Be obsessed with creativity and innovation.
7. They are fact-centric; the more data at their disposal, the better. Be data selective—pay attention to the facts and insights that enable you to do the right things.
8. They grow by doing more and more. Grow by doing less, better.

If your company is suffering from the power of a giant, rank your performance against these tenets of giant slaying. Undoubtedly, you will come up short in some areas. Don't worry. Change won't happen overnight—a shift in corporate culture may be required. Achieving the desired culture is possible, but that won't happen without a strong and tenacious leader at the helm who is passionate about entrepreneurial vision.

Where to Draw the Line

So how do you know when you've gone too far or not far enough on strategic focus and simplicity? How do you know whether you should cut back on services, expand to new areas of businesses, chop the client list, and so forth? There isn't an easy answer to these questions because every business and industry is unique. But two things are certain: firstly, if your business is complex, you have to simplify it. Secondly, if the expansion or the addition is going to create complexity, steer clear of it.

Of course, there is more to this. I'm going to suggest you consider these basic questions and issues when thinking about the expansion or contraction of businesses, services, product lines, brands, clients, customers, geographies, employment, product development, and processes. The list goes on.

1. *Will the contraction improve your strategic well-being?* Example: If I were the purchasing manager for an upscale supermarket chain in search of the highest-quality tomatoes, would I approach the farmer who offers ten different types of produce or the one who grows only tomatoes? If the tomato farmer is actively marketing tomato expertise and has a track record for quality, I would be the perfect target customer, not the retailer interested in average quality, discount-priced tomatoes.

2. *Will the expansion improve efficiencies or scale economies without negating focus?* Companies kid themselves on this one. I can't tell you how many times I've heard this: "Our sales people are already calling on that account. Why not add another line so they can sell more while they are there?" It isn't just about selling. It's about buying, manufacturing, warehousing, shipping, billing, marketing, and culture.

3. *How do you feel about the addition or contraction from a managerial standpoint?* I have met several leaders who are outstanding at managing complexity. Some lead large organizations, while others are one-man shows. But most of us work better when we focus on fewer things. So, as long as your overheads can handle the simplified operation, there is no downside, providing you can grow in the chosen fields of operation.

4. *Are you busy as hell and run off your feet?* If this is the way you want to operate (some will say this is the only way they can operate), there must be a better way. I'm often debating this with my daughter, who is a school vice principal.

She tells me that the educational system is different and that some activities such as report card writing will always be extremely time consuming. She's a remarkable educator, but she's yet to convince me that she can't do less, better.

5. *Think about your business as you might if you were the customer.* Later in the book, I will address the private label industry and the need for flexibility, broad product features, great service, and low cost. This business isn't for me because I'm a value-added branded guy. But for those who excel at efficient manufacturing and pleasing the customer with lowest-cost, readily available goods, the private label co-pack business can be lucrative.

6. *Do you have the expertise to expand, and is your culture conducive to broadening your constituents?* If not, what will it take to shift that culture, and do you really want to do that? These questions need not be answered by those who want to do less, better.

One of the most difficult cuts is the customer list. No one wants to turn down business. I've always admired the advertising agency that resigns a client, especially when the account is well recognized and sizable. My first inclination is that the agency refused to compromise their principles. If that's the truth, I made sure they were on my radar screen.

Chapter 2 Summary

- Strategy is not the *what*, but the *how*. The steel in strategy is the capacity to deliver longer term competitive advantages.
- Be aware of the difference between strategy and tactics.
- The best strategies require sacrifice. They also tell you what not to do.
- Private ownership allows for bold strategic sacrifice. Public ownership almost always postpones it until disaster forces implementation.

- More balls in the air do not present more chances of success in business.
- Every day, market paradigms are shattered by entrepreneurial moves that establish new rules of the game. Lead change and watch your competitors scramble to catch up.
- Clout is the strategy of most giants. The small guy doesn't need deep pockets to coexist with powerful multinationals. Nimbleness, creativity, and culture go a long way.
- Strategic contraction makes you operationally and strategically better. Leverage that competitive advantage with your customers. Instil the right incentives to align your team.

CHAPTER 3

Your Leadership Reality Check

Leaders talk focus all the time, but few deliver the outcomes suggested by the objective. What do increased complexity and incoherence say about the state of twenty-first-century leadership? On the upside, we see or read about superb acts of leadership. The ones that occupy an indelible place in our minds are characterized by unexpected high-pressure, traumatic conditions and courageous actions taken within a very limited amount of time—a cabbie delivering a passenger's baby, a mayor calming a city after one of the worst terrorist attacks in the history of mankind, a pilot making the call to land a powerless 65-ton piece of steel on a river in the middle of a major metropolis, a primary school teacher protecting her class from a gun-wielding madman. With the exception of tampered product recalls, oil spills, and factory explosions, these sorts of trials never face the captains of industry.

Am I implying that leading a business enterprise is easy? Not in the least. But in the context of taking charge and helping human beings escape major and minor crises, every chief executive is blessed with the luxuries of time, subordinate counsel, years of related experience, and know-how imparted by pundits in thousands of books, journals, and case studies.

Yet, twenty-first-century CEOs continue to struggle in their roles as leaders. Only two years ago, the average tenure of a CEO in America was 8.4 years, down from 10.0 years in 2000.[1] According to a Conference Board report, dismissals have been on the rise because of the increased accountability of directors and a greater scrutiny from shareholders and activists. The Conference Board suggests that the pressure of serving as the CEO of a large company in an increasingly competitive global marketplace has resulted in voluntarily shorter tenures, implying that CEOs are leaving on their own terms after fewer years on the job. I'd call this a case of "jumping" before being "pushed."

Stressful, challenging, and sometimes uncontrollable factors come with the corner office. Chief executives are paid big bucks to weave their companies through sick economies, currency fluctuations, and crises. They aren't expected to change the world, but they sure as hell can influence how their companies deal with problems and opportunities. Leaders of well-oiled organizations built on the ethic of strategic sacrifice and a vision that is clear and compelling, sustain competitive advantage by helping others accept change. They understand how to convert ambivalent feelings and snuff out procrastination. Whether a business is large or small, "business as usual" should never exist in the C-suite.

Over my 17-year career in the coffee business, I must have dealt with three or four Brazilian frosts that pushed the price of green coffee futures through the roof. Most of the lessons we learned from these supposedly "uncontrollable factors" were from the errors the executive team made during the first frost—the one that we were ill-prepared for—the one that almost put us out of business. After that calamity, we altered our course during a frost-induced commodity market upswing, knowing how to balance the success prescription of buying, pricing, and selling. In hindsight, the recipe was incredibly simple. We made the best of a difficult situation and always came out of it in much better shape than our competition. You do not throw your hands in the air and tell the shareholders to wait for prices on the commodity market to stabilize.

Sometimes the headway from strategic change doesn't show up on the profit line of the income statement. Progress may be represented by top-line sales, market share, productivity, innovation, new product launches, or expanding distribution. These factors can be the key performance indicators (KPIs) of the organization's well-being. Strategic health ultimately results in profit. But profit can also be the worse indicator of a company's strategic health. Such is the case at the highly prof-itable Campbell Soup Company. Be wary of any business with increasing profits and declining or stagnating sales. Below that shiny profit facade lurks the grim reaper.

With so many books and blogs on leadership, you'd think that people would be sick and tired of the subject. In the printed and digital world, views on leadership command an impressive share of human interest. From their armchairs, American sports buffs witness the impact of great leadership every weekend on high-definition television screens. You cannot watch a National Football League game without hearing references to the leader-ship of coaches and quarterbacks. If you don't give a hoot for sports, there is no shortage of Hollywood dramas and docu-mentaries portraying charismatic individuals defying seemingly impossible odds. Like actors, musicians, and athletes, business leaders have become modern-day celebrities.

Adding to the fascination is the ever-present gap between the-ory and practice. Apparently, the proliferation of self-help books and success stories hasn't done much to guide the leaders of troubled companies that have lost their way. Hewlett-Packard's dismal showing in the boardroom and the corner office is one of the most public leadership fallouts. HP is on their fourth CEO since 2010. I shake my head in bewilderment at the board of directors' inability to find a trailblazer who can set this com-pany on the right course. HP was booted from the Dow in late 2013, and unless current CEO Meg Whitman finds a way to rise above the advance of smartphones, tablets, and cloud comput-ing that continue to punish HPs personal systems business, the company founded in a one-car Palo Alto garage may be another study in shareholders' getting exactly what they deserve.

The irony in this turnaround is the fact that Whitman's pre-decessor recommended to the board that the personal comput-ing business should be divested—that the future of HP lies in software and services, rather than commodity hardware.[2] Any company prepared to kill a $32 billion darling would seemingly be making a significant strategic sacrifice. But this is exactly the kind of thinking that fixes troubled companies. The division contributes 29% of HP's revenue and only 13 percent of its earnings from operations.[3] From my perspective, Whitman is trying to do more of the same, but do it better. Goodbye and good luck.

I like to think of leadership within a competitive context. Leading a company isn't the same as leading less competitive organizations such as academic institutes, charities, civil services, and social associations. I'm not saying business leadership is more difficult. The disparity lies not within the type of organization one leads, but within the particular setting in which leaders ply the tricks of the trade. The conception is clear cut: it is much easier to practice the tenets of good leadership when all is well—when one's side is winning rather than losing. The field of play should not matter.

When your business is bleeding and you've been doing the same old thing, something must change. The person heading an organization on the verge of bankruptcy has to ditch the leadership love-in and step into a crisis management mode. Leading and working in such atmospheres can be awfully tough. In this unenviable territory, patience is not a virtue, nor is job security. This doesn't mean that leaders abdicate the responsibility of illuminating a pathway to heaven. Clarity of purpose, strategy, and vision will never be more critical than in these situations. Mental toughness and tenacity in hard times separate the victors from the vanquished. And it shouldn't matter whether you run a Fortune 500 corporation, a sports team, or the local PTA.

The Seed of Greatness Is Vision

You'd better pay attention to the future because that's where you are going to spend the rest of your life. I don't know who came up with that saying, but suffice to say that foresight is critical to defining futures. The domain that leaders envision must be a better place for their business, their employees, and their customers. When leadership foresight is compelling and inclusive and easily definable, people want to be a part of it; they want to follow their leader to that place. "Easily definable" is the element within visions that facilitates the ethic of simplicity and doing less, better in the complex world of business.

If you look for it, you can find vision in children. Countless times, you must have heard youngsters tell us what they want to be when they grow up. I wanted to be a truck driver. By the time I turned 12, my best friend and I had a completely different idea, but the idea was far from nebulous.

"When Joey and I grow up," I'd say, "we're going to get our own apartment, and we're going to drink beer all week long, and then on Friday, our moms are going to come by and clean up the place so we can start all over again."

As you can imagine, our visionary naiveté had our parents in stiches every time we shared this view of the future. Of course, the prophecy wasn't to last very long. We moved into our aimless teenage years of complication, where we didn't know what we wanted to do or be. This worried my father far more than it worried me, but eventually I found my purpose and that became my compass. As for my father's reaction to this awakening— well, he often shook his head at the transformation—his mind snagged in a contrasting mix of pride and bewilderment. Little Joey's father was on that same train. His son also grew up. Joseph Morin earned a PhD and a professorship at the University of Wisconsin.

Leonardo da Vinci, Ben Franklin, Isaac Newton, Thomas Edison, and Muhammad Ali had visionary grit. The tenacious Socrates believed that the unexamined life was not worth living. Charles Darwin spent 20 years sifting through data, pouring over models, reading, absorbing ideas, and pushing the envelope of understanding. Star Trek creator Gene Roddenberry said, "We must remember that the promise of tomorrow will not be fulfilled easily. The collective commitment of our nations, as well as the vision, wisdom, and hard work of many, many individuals will be required to bring our dreams to fruition. In a way, the Enterprise and the optimistic future in which it exists might be thought of as a reminder of what we can achieve if we try."[4]

Clear visions work for inventors, athletes, sports teams, nations, and companies of all sizes and shapes. The information age has spurred the rise of young entrepreneurs seeking seed money and angel investors for their business ideas. In the old economy, slick merchant bankers and private equity executives sat in oak or mahogany paneled boardrooms listening to slick presentations by blue-suited 40-year-olds. Today's start-up wannabes are 20-year-olds in faded blue jeans carrying rucksacks of ideas, visions, and dreams. You know who they are. Some quickly became renowned billionaire luminaries; many are millionaires. Thousands continue to try, and try again they will. The nutrition that feeds their entrepreneurial lust is vision.

Business is faster and more competitive than ever. And although America finds itself in modest economic recovery, thousands of businesses are filing for bankruptcy—42,008 businesses cut bait in 2012.[5] In October 2013, filings were down, but continued low interest rates have financiers prepared to accept higher risk for higher return by investing in suffering companies that otherwise may have filed. In the long run, companies that fail to operate with a competitive advantage of some type fail to operate.

The choice facing corporate leaders is whether to lead change or scramble to catch up to it. A clear and simple vision is the vital starting point, but that doesn't always guarantee shifts in behavior. Nodding to the premise is easy. Traveling back and forth the fourteen inches between the brain and the heart is the tough part. By converting ambivalent feelings and snuffing out procrastination, leaders can help their followers accept change, emotionally and rationally.

Who Is the Quintessential Twenty-First-Century Leader?

Leaders of the new economy define "tomorrow" beyond the next month, the next quarter, and the next year. The future they envision is the one they choose to create. In their sights is a business "lotus land" that is poles apart from the unwelcoming environment determined by aggressive competitors or bureaucratic regulators. To the surprise of many, their visions are not convoluted; rather, they are specific and generally single minded. They are very good at doing this one thing very well. The result, not the objective, is the financial consequence of the lotus land they envisioned in the first place.

Failure to operate within this mind-set or to take the obligatory action to move toward "the dream" inevitably draws companies and their leaders into the dreadful pit of defensiveness. Defensiveness leads to complexity when leaders and followers scramble to buoy up the income statement's top line. Complexity is a poor substitute for vision.

Microsoft has been adept at the vision game for more than a quarter of a century. Google's Larry Page and Sergey Brin are two others who make big bets on the big, breakthrough dreams, not small incremental improvements. Google's mission of "Organizing the world's information and making it universally accessible and useful"[6] is simple. What an incredibly effective way to express a dream. Little more than a decade of web brilliance, and this highly profitable company is generating $60 billion in revenues and growing in leaps and bounds.

Bill Gates, Larry Page, and Sergey Brin were in tune with the environments in which their companies would operate, but never fretted the less desirable influences. A few nasty years of economic woe in America and Europe could not dampen either company's zeal for phenomenal growth. That's because success hinged on the strategic choices these visionaries made—they cut through the clutter and pinpointed the markets, the products, and the applications in which to make their wagers.

Yes, entrepreneurial foresight is alive and well within the information age companies, but it is not limited to the techs. You've probably never heard of Hamdi Ulukaya. I hadn't either until I watched an episode of *Rock Center* with Brian Williams. Journalist Harry Smith interviewed this Turkish farmer who arrived in America to acquire an education and to learn business. Ulukaya learned a lot more than that. He discovered that the cheese Americans consumed was mediocre, and the yogurt was horrid. Seven years later, Ulukaya was in the cheese business, supplying feta to New York's specialty retailers.

When he heard that Kraft was selling a century-old yogurt plant, a vision of what could be, began to percolate. Why in the world wouldn't Americans embrace an unmistakably superior product? Unable to shake the entrepreneurial possibilities, he borrowed the money and bought Kraft's brick and mortar for a few cents on the dollar. Within five years, Chobani Greek Yogurt was firmly profitable and on the verge of surpassing a billion dollars in annual sales. The sailing wasn't smooth. A business growing at 65 percent annually will face considerable challenges, but most of Ulukaya's had to do with operations and, surprisingly, not the onslaught of competitive response. If Chobani were your business, would say you were in the yogurt business or the dairy business? If your answer is the yogurt business, you've made a worthwhile strategic sacrifice.

Ten years into the future, the social, political, economic, and technological environment will be very different. Successful CEOs will deal with the challenges of novel landscapes and continue to lead the march forward with unencumbered compelling visions, insightful strategies, and applications that may cause them to stumble from time to time, but never fall.

By stick-handling through the dynamic terrain of the future, they will incisively pinpoint, and fervently deploy the critical success factors of the company and industry in which they operate. This raises the question of whether the definition of leadership is set for a change. I think not. As with any other era in the history of corporations, the range of personal attributes required of a CEO must align with the type and state of affairs of the enterprise in which they ply their trade. Is a "turnaround" artist right for a profitable bureaucracy? Can a great, entrepreneurial-driven "start-up" CEO steer a mature organization? Are shareholders looking for a builder or a banker?

Twenty-First-Century Fishponds

Great leaders don't allow shifting environments to negatively impact performance. This applies to business, social, economic, and technological change. As the century's fishpond unfolds, great leaders will figure out how to swim around every vortex of challenge with strategies that are right for their business and for their customers.

No matter how good your crystal ball, you are going to be surprised by the future. Here's my take on that future:

1. *Business will be more complex.* Sorry, I know that's rather obvious. Computers were supposed to make things easier for us. Partly true. They also pumped out a plethora of data. I know from my experience in marketing that the human brain can absorb only so much information, and of that, a small percentage is retained. Today's Web offers a bottomless pit of instant data. How many years would you need to read every Wikipedia post? The finite number doesn't matter. You are going to be reading for a long, long time. Imagine what lies ahead. Not to worry, though. The trick is to determine relevancy. The consummate

entrepreneurial leader does less better by making the decision with 80 percent of the information in hand, rather than spending boundless hours searching for the 20 percent obscured by the bush.

2. *C-suite executives will be time starved.* You are likely thinking they are already time starved. But it is going to get worse, even with advances in communications technology. Shifting markets and shareholder pressures will escalate. To meet top-line goals and earnings expectations, companies will have to sell more of their goods to the same domestic customers and attract heaps of new customers in foreign lands. China will be opportunity number one. I was shocked when I learned that China's Internet users were pegged at 538 million in June 2012—that's almost double the population of the United States.[7] Sadly, the hours in the day for C-suite executives will still max out at 24.

3. *Expect forward integration to accelerate.* Farmers are circumventing grocery stores by taking their fruits and vegetables to local markets. PepsiCo and Coca-Cola have been buying their bottlers for greater control and cost savings. Manufacturers, who are under the thumbs of formidable traditional retailers and continue to fret about losing product listings, need a siren wake-up call. Because of the social network and the ease of buying from a computer or a smartphone, online shopping is gnawing away at conventional retailing. Every retailer has an online strategy, some because they have to, others because they want to. As for the endangered species known as wholesalers and distributors, to these middlemen I bid them a sad farewell.

4. *Employees will demand balanced lives.* Marketers that help people achieve balance through relevant products and services will reap substantial commercial rewards. No doubt, this quest for equilibrium will affect labor strategies.

Employers who seize the opportunity to satisfy employees' needs will rediscover loyalty in their workforce and benefit from greater productivity. To me, that's a sacrifice well worth making.

5. *Corporate social responsibility will be a given.* Failure to join the fight to save the planet will bring on a storm of consumer backlash and excessive tax penalties. Insightful CEOs will lead the charge, and many are already onto this earnest initiative—their companies standing out among the public as models of good corporate citizenry. In the final analysis, who better to be the chief custodian of the all-important corporate brand than the chief executive?

6. *Industry consolidation will turn on its end.* Mega companies will be broken up into smaller pieces for many reasons, the most important being the need to regain strategic and operational control. However, this was not Kraft's reason for splitting their behemoth into a Kraft grocery division and a snacks division named Mondelez. I fail to see a trace of brilliance in the Mondelez nomenclature, especially in light of the fact that Kraft had some terrific trademarks in their stable, such as Cadbury, Nabisco, and Suchard. Make no mistake. The split at Kraft was nothing more than a stock market play. For others, who want to increase shareholder value the old-fashioned way, the significance of regaining singularity of purpose and reducing operational and strategic complexity has never been so vital.

7. Although shopping from home will continue its remarkable escalation, *working from home will not grow as much as expected.* Regardless of roadway congestion and the quest for balance in life, working away from the office will have to compete with the power of teamwork within the walls of brick and mortar. Face-to-face interaction will remain an integral spoke in the competitive advantage wheel. So will the flexible work week that is necessary to enable this

evolution. But with mobile Internet traffic expected to surpass desktop traffic, more and more consumers will enjoy the convenience of shopping anywhere and anytime.

How leaders view environmental change and what they do about it determines their downstream destiny. The "doom and gloom" theorists, who constantly whine about the challenges of the new economy, are polluting the human capital of their organizations. Unlike energetic leaders keen to influence the future, these sad sacks have lost their footing on the slippery slope of demise. Regardless of market or economic conditions, achievers prioritize and exercise the principles of great leadership. A well-crafted, genuine manifesto can be the formidable guiding light of clarity and cohesion.

Manifesto Potency

Manifestos are the visions that ignite hearts and souls, inspiring people to act. The greatest manifestos, such as the Ten Commandments and the Declaration of Independence, are so potent that their catalytic effects have endured for centuries. As recently as 50 years ago, an emotional speech delivered from the steps of the Lincoln Memorial established a convincing and undeniable purpose for civil rights in America. Today, Martin Luther King's "I Have a Dream" speech is arguably the most inspiring manifesto of the past century.

Even though manifestos generally apply to political movements, the ideals and intent of such powerful texts in industry can also cause people to excel on behalf of the organizations and the people that employ them. A couple of years ago, I had the pleasure of helping Houweling's Tomatoes of Camarillo, California, develop a manifesto. One hundred and seventy-five acres under glass makes Houweling's one of the largest greenhouse tomato producers in North America.

I'll use the words of founder and CEO Casey Houweling to explain. "When we started working on the project, we quickly concluded that Houweling's manifesto would never be a stereotypical vision statement. It would represent who we are, what we do, and what we believe in. I'm not one to pound my chest or set a pie-in-the-sky goal that employees will see as unreachable. Anyway, to make a long story short, John and I decided to base our manifesto on the true values of Houweling's—culturally, we should continue to do what we are doing and continue learning to be ourselves. Mastery is a powerful word around here. One never reaches mastery, and that is fine with me as long as we never stop reaching for it."

The Houweling's manifesto: "Do What You Love. Love What You Do. We Grow Tomatoes in Glass Houses. *Mastery Under Glass* is Our Mindset, Our Personal Quest to Carefully Harmonize the Art and Science of Greenhouse Farming. *Mastery Under Glass* Doesn't Come Easily. You Need Perseverance. Passion. Respect for the Earth. This Ethic is in Casey Houweling's Blood. This Ethic Inspires Us to Produce the Best Tomatoes in the World."

I'm going to break down the discipline of this manifesto as it applies to sacrifice and simplicity. At the outset, Casey defines his core business as tomatoes. I suspect there's not a week that goes by when the thought of expanding the line doesn't enter his mind. But to his credit, he sticks with his core, even though customers continue to ask for various types of sweet bell peppers. The construction of a new third tomato greenhouse operation in Utah is proof of sticking to the knitting. Specialists beat generalists, but to enjoy that strategic advantage, they have to pass on new businesses from time to time.

Produce is a very tough industry in the United States and Canada. Shelf life is short. Every retailer wants a lower price. Loyalty is hard to come by. Overripe fruit that has to be destroyed is an outrageous cost—the farmer loses the sale, and his productivity per acre plummets. When one watches tons of fruit going to waste, it would be easy to relax the quality standards, just a tiny bit. But when the values of "best quality, respect for the earth, mastery, and passion," are embedded in your manifesto, sacrificing quality for productivity is wickedness.

This doesn't mean that the folks at Houweling's don't give a hoot for productivity. On the contrary, productivity is right up there with quality. This ethic requires a sacrifice. That sacrifice is the owner's pocketbook—significant investments in technologies that increase quality and reduce cost are the investments that Casey Houweling is willing to make.

Lululemon Athletica is a self-described yoga-inspired apparel company, which produces athletic clothing and operates 200 stores in the United States, Canada, Australia, and New Zealand. Their manifesto is a list of 31 ideas and philosophies on life. Some examples: Do one thing a day that scares you; 10–15 friends allow for real friendship; what you do to the earth you do to yourself; stress is related to 99 percent of all illnesses.[8] Lululemon's goal is to create a distinctive staff culture and a set of values that permeate right through to the customer. Buy something at Lululemon and you will find the manifesto printed on the stylish shopping bag that holds the apparel you have purchased. Thirty-one life philosophies sound like a lot to absorb, but the sum of the parts makes clear the Lululemon way.

Crafting a company manifesto is no easy task. This checklist should help.

1. *State a Compelling Purpose*. The better ones define their products, their services, and their company's deep emotional principles.
2. *Capture Core Values*. Core values *are* Lululemon's manifesto. Houweling's manifesto connects the values to the product.
3. *Be Honest*. Mission statements are full of elaborate words and illusionary tomorrows. Great manifestos incite human emotions when they are true.

4. *Link Business Life to Personal Life.* Tech missions and manifestos tend to shy away from this. There is good reason,
   because unlike in most industries, tech life and home life
   are intertwined. Lululemon takes the notion a step further
   by staying true to their values objective. They do not talk
   about their brand; instead, they talk about you.

5. *Be Inclusive.* A manifesto must touch (and move) everybody. I don't know whether Disney, Nike, Cirque du Soleil,
   or the New England Patriots have a manifesto. But they
   sure as hell act like they do.

6. *Always Differentiate.* There is nothing more powerful than
   admirable differentiation in competitive arenas. That goes
   for business and sports...even war.

The fact that outgoing Lululemon CEO Christine Day spent
20 years at Starbucks might explain why she is a proponent of
potent cultures. At an investor conference in mid-2013, she
declared that the Lululemon culture would more than survive
her departure. It would thrive.

"I am not the culture of Lululemon," she said emphatically.
"Everyone is the culture of Lululemon."[9] Continued volume and
profit increases seem to back that up. So does the fact the company is more than halfway to its target of having 300 Lululemon
stores in the United States.

Unlike the stereotypical corporate mission or vision statement, a potent manifesto says who you are, what you believe in,
and why you should be prepared to invest of yourself in a particular cause. When everyone is on board and living the ideals,
it is awfully hard to wander off the track.

The Ultimate Leadership Test

Have you ever considered what might be your greatest leadership
test? As you contemplate the question, a number of scenarios

may leap to mind, including layoffs within your department, the sudden death of an employee, disastrous new product launches, horrific dips in market share, or departures of key people to your competition. Do any of these trials and tribulations touch a nerve? How about the sudden, unexpected, and potentially catastrophic event that threatens the entire enterprise?

Not too many years ago, the entire world was rocked by the most environmentally destructive business crisis of all time—BP's horrific oil spill in the Gulf. Everyone watched as CEO Tony Hayward made blunder after blunder while BP's crude destroyed life. Three weeks after the explosion, Hayward called the spill "relatively tiny" in comparison with the size of the ocean—six weeks later he said he'd like his life back, and six weeks after that, BP's shell-shocked board finally released him from his despair. Here was a guy who would not make the required sacrifices.

How is it possible for three months of crisis management incompetence to occur in an organization the size of BP, whose product is ecologically toxic? You'd think a wealthy company drilling on the ocean's floor would be adept at risk management planning. Whether Hayward was part of a risk management plan or not, the guy failed at a time when his employees, his shareholders, his fellow human beings, and the planet needed him most.

Kaitlin Roig and Chesley "Sully" Sullenberger did not fail when called upon. Kaitlin was the 29-year-old first-grade teacher who hurried her class into a tiny bathroom at the sound of gunfire at Sandy Hook Elementary. She then pulled a bookshelf in front of the door to barricade them in. As she waited for either the gunman or the liberator, she went about comforting her students by telling them how much she loved them.

Sullenberger, the pilot of US Airways Flight 1549, managed to land a powerless air bus on the Hudson River off midtown Manhattan. Cool and calm under incredible pressure, this man saved the lives of all 155 occupants with his courage and resolve.

Compared to these two acts of courage, a business crisis should be a cakewalk for the organization's leader. Those who excel under fire do so because of several factors, the most important of which, I have listed below:

1. *They have the right values and beliefs.* Great leaders live by a set of principles that guide them when the need arises.
2. *They are inherently courageous.* There is not an absence of fear in these individuals, but rather the ability to manage fear. Anyone who has overcome intense fright will tell you that there isn't a greater rush.
3. *They are prepared to make a personal sacrifice and put their own interests last.* Their organizations are disciplined to assess threats and map ways to mitigate and to deal with the potentiality. The CEO has to believe the disaster will come, and when it does, the company will be prepared to cope from the moment the crisis occurs to the point that recovery procedures begin.
4. *They know how to communicate.* Getting the right ideas into the heads of others is paramount. In the case of a recall or an environmental catastrophe, the first concern is public safety, not the financial interests of the shareholders. I am going to repeat that. The first concern is public safety, not the financial interests of the shareholders.
5. *They live and breathe the company's values.* If the culture is right, the decision-making is so much easier.

Shortly after I became CEO of Jacobs Suchard, the company shipped a massive batch of sour-tasting coffee nationwide. Consumer complaints skyrocketed, and some people reported nausea. This was to become my ultimate leadership test. As CEO, I was guided by our company's culture and values during this difficult time.

Out came the crisis management manual that our management team had prepared, updated, and reviewed annually. The
pages detailed what to do and how to do it. But like most crises,
every situation is unique. Our issue sure wasn't black and white.
The facts were as follows:

- More than 90 percent of the production run that was shipped
  turned out to be untainted. But because the coffee was ground
  and vacuum packed, we had no way of determining the good from
  the bad without destroying every package of the entire batch, in
  the process watching millions of dollars go down the drain.
- Exacerbating the predicament was the fact that the tainted product was not toxic. No one was going to die by drinking it or
  taking a sip. I'd describe the severity of the fouled product as
  analogous to milk that was in the initial stages of "going off."
- Most people said there was somewhat of a sour taste. A fraction
  of a percent said the coffee actually made them vomit. Like I
  said, the crisis wasn't exactly a clear case of black and white.

Now for another twist and some added complexity—a problem percolated in the Jacobs Suchard boardroom. Our fiscal
year was six weeks from completion, and we were on track to
overachieve the budgeted profit. The snag was the fellow to
whom I reported in the Zurich head office. I judged him as a
mercenary whose number one priority was his annual bonus. I
was deeply concerned that when I informed him of the crisis,
he would swing the board to either delay a recall until the next
fiscal or approve a partial, rather than complete recall in order
that we would deliver the profit target. I couldn't live with either
outcome. The tainted coffee had to come back to our roasting
facility. So, rather than roll the dice on what posture he might
take, I made the multimillion-dollar decision to issue a national
recall on my own, without his or the board's knowledge of the
sour coffee problem. Once the recall was public and underway,
I gave him the news. By issuing a national recall, I had forfeited

the annual budgeted profit. That was the first of three sacrifices I made at that stressful time.

Despite my belief that this move was morally and commercially correct, I had committed insubordination, thereby putting my neck on the line—that was sacrifice number two. And I came damn close to losing my job over this. But when the dust cleared, I emerged from the crisis with my heart still beating. Sacrifice number three was my bonus and everyone else's.

Now for the part that warmed the cockles of my heart— none of the senior or the middle management team resented sacrificing their bonus for the higher cause. That is a cultural testament.

This crisis required countless hours of communication with several stakeholder groups, not the least of which were government health officials. The folks I dealt with couldn't have cared less for Jacobs Suchard. Notwithstanding the moral obligation, I was going to do everything in my power to protect the reputation of the company. If the company's and/or the brand's reputation suffered, so would business and employment. In the end, we got through that sour coffee crisis without a damaged image or a loss of market share. As for how I handled myself as a leader, my feelings are the same today as they were all those years ago. I loved every minute of it. Why? Because that crisis gave me the opportunity to be the leader my employees expected, and the leader I'd always dreamed of becoming.

Get Your Hands Dirty

Companies need leaders who are prepared to invest their time advancing the business model or finding a revolutionary new model to add value. "Advancing the model" is just another way of saying improving or fortifying competitive advantages. One doesn't have to be a CEO to make a worthy leadership contribution. The catalyst for action at any level of the organization is a shared purpose. Is that purpose clear and inspiring? Is the strategy capable of delivering it? The strategy, like the vision, also has to be clear and concise.

But strategies are useless without execution. Leaders must ask themselves whether their corporate culture is conducive to the proper execution of the strategy. Assuming there is a disconnect, would you expect the leadership team to change the strategy or change the culture?

A few years ago, J.C. Penney recruited the former head of Apple's retail operations as their savior. Known as the man responsible for the aggressive expansion of Apple's retail outlets a decade earlier, Ron Johnson came to Penney's corner office with superb credentials. Right away, he replaced several executives, including the chief operating officer (COO), the CMO, and the chief technology officer (CTO). He believed J.C. Penney's number one competitor was the company itself.

"The way you unlock potential," he said, "is to find a new way to compete, ideally in a way that's never been done before, so it's seen as new. Our number two competitor is everyone else."[10]

As it turned out, Johnson's big play wasn't new, nor was it breakthrough or innovative. Certainly it was bold, and in his mind, strategically essential. He eliminated all the bargain sales and went with everyday low prices, figuring the move would be meaningful and motivational to Penney's consumers. It was not. By the end of 2012, same-store sales and traffic had headed south. Johnson was already asking his board for more time. At that stage, Penney's directors had little choice but to grant it, but not for long. Four months later, Johnson was out. It is no wonder. Retail sales had declined by 25 percent. This rocket man had misunderstood Penney's customers and gambled big on one errant roll of the dice.

What sacrifices did he make? Perhaps some sleepless nights once it became clear that the strategy had backfired and so had the board's confidence in his leadership.

Innovation starts with asking questions. Insight progresses to disruptive hypotheses. Insight can come from anywhere—your colleagues, your customers, your spouse, even your kids. Depending on the leader and the organization, there are a host of ways to draw it out—some arduous, others as easy as seeing a simple headline on a billboard and converting the idea into a viable business concept. When I was in the corner office, I institutionalized three seemingly minor initiatives that created some results. Many of these thoughts improved my performance as a leader and enhanced the company's competitive position. You don't have to be the top dog of a corporation to enjoy similar advantages. All you have to do is maintain a link to the action and the grassroots of the enterprise. The three little steps are the following:

1. One day per year, my management team donned overalls and worked side by side with our union employees in the factories. We joined them for the coffee break and lunch, and chatted about the company, their roles, their hobbies, and their families. Giving up a day of office time is a tiny sacrifice. I finished my shift with new insights. Our plant workers loved the fact that I was willing to "get my hands dirty with them." I didn't realize it at the time, but years later, I came to understand that in their minds, this act humanized me. If you don't have a factory, work the cash register or the call center or the warehouse or...

2. Make a point of personally handling customer complaints. I made a company-wide commitment to personally handle one complaint per day. In addition to dealing with the customer's problem, this empathetic interface gave me the chance to have a conversation about our products and services. Occasionally, I got an earful, but by the time I apologized, suggested how I might rectify the issue, and thanked the irate consumer for his or her time, I had a happy, loyal

customer and a deeper personal insight. Now, consider the impact that my hands-on involvement had on the company's customer service ethic.

3. Spend a day with a sales representative. By no means does this preclude annual top-to-top meetings with senior executives of the largest and/or most important business-to-business customers. A day with a sales person in a remote location serves two purposes. Firstly, it opens a leader's mind to issues and opportunities from the distant front line. Secondly, it sends a message to the entire sales force that the senior executive cares about salespeople and values their input, as well as the ideas of the customer.

For me, these initiatives began with a mission to advance the business model. The result was far greater. Three small steps turned into one giant leap that garnered insight, humanized a CEO, and fortified the corporate culture. I recommend that every member of the C-suite get his or her hands dirty, disrupt the status quo, and champion innovation within his or her department and the organization.

When Business Sours, Don't Panic

"Don't throw the baby out with the bathwater" is the saying advising us not to discard something valuable in our eagerness to get rid of some useless thing associated with it. Without prudent leadership, this can happen to companies going through a rough patch.

In terms of rectification, you have to look at the issue in the context of whether the problem is a short-term blip or the beginning of a long-term strategic shift in your industry. In the coffee business, for example, a spike in coffee futures from a serious frost in South America will elevate the selling price of coffee and reduce customer demand. This is a short-term aggravation, and although it may thrash earnings for the quarter or even the year, it is not a fundamental restructuring of the marketplace. An experienced company that deals in commodities understands the ramifications and addresses the challenges that come with this type of business. Knowledgeable management has seen these hiccups before, and they'll see them again. Management may circle the wagons to some degree, but they should avoid slashing strategic programs that are in place to enhance their mid- to long-term relationship with the customer.

If your company is going through such challenges, do not panic. Sure, it isn't status quo business, and yes, every CEO has to make some moves to shore up profits. Tighten your belt, but rethink the generic quick fixes. Do not make across-the-board cuts. Leaders justify pervasive cost-cutting because they think it is the fair thing to do; they also don't want to sacrifice their popularity.

Across-the-board cuts may be fair, but they aren't smart. When it comes to belt-tightening, prudent leaders and managers sacrifice those areas or projects that do not detract from the core strategy or the company's competitive differentiation. When I was in the corner office, I managed to squirrel away a "rainy day" fund for nasty business blips.

I was never a big fan of cents-off couponing because too much of it can become habitual. You buy the customer with a discount price, and the customer grows dependent on that price, (and so do you). From time to time, we did issue modest cents-off coupons, and with this came a "coupon reserve" account for redemptions that would take the better part of a year to find their way to our accounts payable group. The KPMGs of the world love these reserve accounts because they don't want nasty surprises in companies that might artificially deflate the longer-term redemption estimate to improve the shorter-term annual profit. In our particular case, the opposite occurred. We made generous estimates of coupon redemptions because we were delivering against our profit objectives. The difference in a 5 percent estimate and an 8 percent estimate of redemption could be hundreds of thousands of dollars depending on the face value of the coupon. The surplus became our rainy day fund, and with that safety net in place, I never had to compromise my strategic principles. (For the record, the surplus was grossly inadequate to fund that national coffee recall.)

Avoid trashing strategic initiatives that are working. Having grown up in the branded consumer goods industry, I've seen many a case of cuts to the advertising budget. One can certainly justify the axe when a campaign's efficacy is in doubt—far better to pull that campaign, stop putting good media money into bad creative, and start working on better, more persuasive advertising. Fortunately, in today's social media world, massive budgets aren't necessarily required to effectively engage consumers. Yet, in cases where budgets are tiny, there is strategic risk to cutbacks. Sadly, the reward of the savings in social media is a drop in the proverbial corporate bucket—a diminutive sum in propping up quarterly or annual earnings.

Knee-jerk reactions to the core strategy itself are unforgivable. Only when the rough patch is a sea change in the marketplace should corporate leaders tackle the corporate strategy. I'm talking about big change such as Amazon's impact on conventional book retailers and iPhone's blow to the Blackberry. A price squeeze from oversupply and weaker demand can be incredibly irritating. Again, don't panic. Avoid throwing the Hail Mary pass. Understand the reason for the problem. Deal with it, sooner rather than later.

Is the setback self-inflicted? Do you have the right people in place to minimize the ramifications or to lead you out of the short-term trouble? Seldom are people to blame. But these glitches have a way of distinguishing good leaders from bad.

When business goes sour, be it in the short- or the long-term, the organization's most senior people need to step up, choose their sacrifices carefully, and offer innovative solutions to the elements hammering the top- and the bottom line. Those who fail to do this are not leaders. At best, they are managers. At worst, they are expendable.

Are Great CEOs Great Leaders?

Leaders with an insatiable zeal to create a new market with a unique technology or a breakthrough product generally make great CEOs. This obsession is rooted in their desire to define their company's place in the future; they can't stomach the thought of reacting to a future created by their competitors. In theory, the principles and personal characteristics that constitute great leadership should accompany the traits of greats CEOs. But this isn't always the case. Here's why:

1. By definition, people who fail to deliver quantitative business results for the companies they lead are not great CEOs (of that company). That does not preclude an individual from becoming a great leader and a great CEO elsewhere. John Scully, an astute leader, was considered the top of his class during his years leading PepsiCo. Then he moved to Apple and failed miserably. Same leader, different result.
2. Companies, markets, and the categories in which they compete can be exceedingly dissimilar. Fundamentally, the leadership style or the skill set required of a CEO in one environment may be the kiss of death in another.
3. CEOs can exhibit some weird leadership characteristics and still manage to get the job done. Would Apple have been anywhere near as successful had Steve Jobs not been ruthless, impatient, emotional, stubborn, intense, and controlling?

No one knows the answer to that question, but I'll venture a guess. Apple would not have been as successful without Jobs, not so much because of his weaknesses, but because of his strengths. In his particular case, his difficult leadership style did not stand in the way of corporate success, but it surely inhibited the personal success of many people who worked for him. I say that because those who suffered the wrath of Jobs defined success differently. Those who quit weren't prepared to make the sacrifices that his style of leadership demanded.

The most important question a CEO must answer is, "What should we do?" Once he or she has taken care of that, the next question is, "How should we do it?" This brings me back to the strategic options: Are we going to do more with more? Are we going to do more with less? Are we going to do less, better?

Bold Leadership

A couple of years ago I read a book about RAF fighter pilots in World War II. One particular passage stood out. It was this: "There are old fighter pilots and bold fighter pilots, but there are no old, bold fighter pilots." The book's author, a fighter pilot himself, was making the point that the very best dogfighters were young, because of superb eyesight and lightning reflexes. What do fighter pilots have to do with the world of business? Is it that their courage could surely come in handy in the C-suite?

Kidding aside, the point is this: we generally think of the word "bold" as a very positive character trait. Be careful. "Bold" should never stand on its own, nor should "bold" ever be singular. We don't want airlines, oil riggers, and gas pipeline distributors acting bold. We know the downside of this corporate behavior. We've witnessed the effects of BP's oil spill in the Gulf, and some of us remember the Chernobyl nuclear disaster. Caution is the operative word.

But in no way should this discount the power of boldness. Bold needs a qualifier, a partner. Donald Trump is bold. So is Howard Schultz. These guys are as different as night and day. Trump could be thought of as a bold narcissist. By contrast, Schultz is strategically bold, entrepreneurially bold, and imaginatively bold. He's been that way for 35 years. His boldness works like a charm for his customers, his employees, and his shareholders.

In business, "bold" needs a partner. I like these five cohorts:

1. *Strategic Boldness.* Legendary adman Leo Burnett liked to say, "When you reach for the stars you may not quite get one, but you won't come up with a handful of mud either."[11] Burnett was encouraging his staff to always strive for greatness. If you want to do less, better, make sure your strategy isn't wishy-washy and open to interpretation. Tight strategies tell everyone what not to do.

2. *Bold Entrepreneurship.* Sorry, folks. This is a bit of a given. I've never seen a successful entrepreneur known for cautiousness. Have you? Bold entrepreneurs sacrifice security.

3. *Bold Innovation.* The bolder you are in the search for innovation, the more likely you are to unearth the big idea and get it into the market. Tom Peter's "ready, fire, aim" chant continues to prevail. Try it, adapt it, and then get it right.

4. *Bold Visions.* You'll never find a breakthrough idea for your business if your goal is to modestly increase sales, say, by 5 percent. Think 100 percent increases. Which of these two targets has the best chance of delivering a 50 percent increase? You don't get 50 percent by fine-tuning.

5. *Bold and Virtuous Leadership.* Honor and honesty not only strengthen a bold leader but impact every follower and make the effort meaningful.

Chapter 3 Summary

- Every challenging environment presents tremendous opportunities for leaders to excel. Maintaining clarity and cohesion through the tough times differentiates the victors from the vanquished.

- Farsightedness is essential to effective leadership. Clear, compelling visions set the stage for growth.
- Transformational leaders sacrifice the security of the status quo. Will you lead change or scramble to catch up?
- Innovation insight isn't limited to information technology organizations. Ideas and creativity are waiting to be unleashed at every level in every organization.
- Practice and embrace the power of listening.
- Carefully prepared, genuine manifestos tell everyone who you are, what you believe in, and why your cause is worth the sacrifice.
- Don't think that all great CEOs are great leaders.
- Boldness is not enough. Link it to strategy, innovation, entrepreneurship, vision, and virtuous leadership.

CHAPTER 4

The Urgency for Action

The French author Andre Maurois said, "Business is a combination of war and sport."[1] Among several notions, including the importance of strategy and tactics, Maurois was alluding to the premise that those engaged in war despise their enemy. In business, your competitor is the enemy. Hugo Powell, an outstanding leader who preceded me in the corner office at Jacobs Suchard, reportedly lived by the credo that to achieve success in sales and profit, the other guy had to fail. The truth of the matter was that Hugo was a skilled turnaround expert recruited to save a failing business on the brink of bankruptcy. When a company is in the red because of smart competitive maneuvers or its own ineptitude, disdain for the competition rises to the surface. This happens to be the psyche of leaders in a "turn-around" mode. Desperate times require desperate measures. Our cause was survival—personally and professionally. The thing that stood in our way was the competition. As in war, a common enemy unifies and motivates one's own army behind a mutually beneficial cause. Neither Hugo nor those of us who served as his vice-presidents could stomach the tarnishing of our business reputations that would come with the demise of the company or our dismissals to make way for the next turnaround team.

After the renewal in Canada and a brief stint in Germany, Hugo resigned from Jacobs Suchard and went on to lead Labatt Breweries and later Labatt's parent, Belgium-based InterBrew, now Anheuser-Busch InBev. His leadership style never changed, and the beer maker's shareholders ought to be damn glad of it. Hugo made them a whack of money and a pretty pile for himself when he stepped down as CEO. I was extremely fortunate to have worked under Hugo. I have yet to meet a better strategist or a more competitive executive.

Ever heard of eyewear maker Luxottica? I hadn't until I came upon this company in my research for this book. Luxottica is a $7 billion enterprise that manufactures glasses for several high-end brands such as Coach, Ralph Lauren, Chanel, Prada, and Tiffany, as well as their own brands, Oakley and Ray-Bans. Luxottica also owns 7,000 stores around the globe under several retail banners, including LensCrafters, Sunglass Hut, and Pearl Vision.[2]

Luxottica's strategy of controlling the value chain from production all the way to consumer sales and service has created a stranglehold on the market. By freezing out competition, they can sell frames and lenses at 20 times the cost of production.

Luxottica is the enemy of Warby Parker, an online start-up unified by a worthy mission. Hell-bent on showing the eyewear world a better way, Warby Parker's strategy avoids middlemen and attacks the big guy's weakness—ridiculously high prices. Warby Parker's niche is boutique-quality eyewear for $120.00 . . . and for every pair sold, a second pair will go to someone in need, at no cost. You get a sense of their rebellious personality and their dislike for the big guys from their website.[3] They spell out the customer's problem—that prescription eyewear should not cost $300+. They explain why the problem exists—highly concentrated industries inflate prices to generate huge profits from customers who have no other options. And finally, they tell us how they are solving the problem—by circumventing traditional channels and offering boutique-quality eyewear through their website at a fraction of the price.

Despite the clout of Luxottica, Warby Parker appears to be doing rather well within their defined niche. This isn't an example of specialist versus generalist, but rather niche specialist versus mass specialist—eyewear being the category domain. Because both companies operate with powerful competitive advantages, coexistence is probable for years to come, barring a takeover by Luxottica.

For most of my career, I operated within intense arenas where fractions of market share points translated into millions of dollars. The companies that employed me were generally market underdogs waging warfare against bigger, better-financed organizations. Against mounting odds, these underdogs flourished. Competitive situations shape distinct individual and team behaviors. If your senses are stirred by the following six characteristics that constitute this type of culture, then you and I are kindred spirits:

1. *An intellect of urgency.* This is a tremendous plus for the smaller player. Nimbleness and urgency to get the job done will set you apart from your competitors in so many ways, particularly with customers.
2. *Well-articulated goals.* Like a sports scorecard, competitive spirit demands performance measurement and accountability. Your success or failure can be quantified by such key business indicators as market share, financial ratios, brand awareness, new product launches, and execution within the deadlines.
3. *Innovation-driven headsets.* Only an idiot wants to compete in a financial spitting contest. You cannot outspend a giant with a fat balance sheet. Rather, you must outsmart the giant with entrepreneurial thinking, brilliant ideas, and impeccable execution.
4. *Zero tolerance for complacency.* Even when you pull ahead, run up the score. Never give the enemy an even break. Increase your lead, and while they scramble to catch you, unleash the next breakthrough product, service, or promotion.
5. *Intimate knowledge of the adversary.* You must know how your opponents think, corporately and individually. Study their moves. Keep a journal and continually update it and share it with your colleagues. Go ahead, dislike the

competition. But don't be so obsessed with their demise that you allow yourself to be drawn into egotistical price wars. Yes, there are times when you will have to respond to aggression by trimming your margins. But winning a price war, no matter the cost, signals that you have lost your appreciation of the business objectives. All you have to do is make your rivals *think* you are prepared to win at any cost. That's why you have to respond from time to time.

6. *Focus on the things that matter.* By concentrating on preemptive projects within your control, you can keep the enemy on their heels. Isn't that a lot more fun than backtracking and scampering away in retreat?

Resting on your laurels is the Achilles heel of dominance. Companies become complacent in markets that are devoid of rivalry. Look at BlackBerry. Five years ago, BlackBerry was synonymous with smartphones. Then along came formidable competition with mobiles that delivered superior customer benefits. Today, BlackBerry is struggling to survive. This is a stunning fall from grace considering that this company, once known as Research In Motion, pioneered push email with devices that were considered so indispensable that their product was nicknamed Crack-Berry. It is not as if BlackBerry was operating in a noncompetitive landscape. They either didn't realize it or they had no idea how to handle the competitive onslaught. BlackBerry10 (Z10) was the latest Hail Mary pass. Sadly, for BlackBerry there were no receivers in the end zone to haul in the ball.

To win the game of market share, one side has to tip the scales better than the others. With only 100 percent available to the players and with the availability of quick data, it isn't long before you know whether your play(s) has been effective or not. That's exhilarating.

Stop right there. There just might be a dangerous delusion in this scenario. Is market share growth the "be all and end all" of success? Does dominant market share create competitive advantage because of marketplace power and scale economies? This used to be true. In some industries the market share notion continues to prevail, but this is the mentality of the old guard. Old economy thinking works within known market space defined by industry boundaries and competitive rules. The 100 percent market share boundary can get awfully crowded, with a lot of players getting caught up in defending their territory. Without prudence, a zealous market share proponent can succumb to tactics, many of which are ill-defined. Sure, short-term discounting can protect or spike market share. Medium- to long term, it hammers profits. For the consumer packaged goods industry, cents-off couponing and deep discounts have become the crack cocaine of brand promotion.

The new guard doesn't operate this way. Yes, they work hard at improving their competitive positions within existing markets. But they are also farsighted. As with Nespresso, Nestlé's horizon was a new market, but a market that was a natural extension within their core brand's (Nescafé) scope of expertise—coffee. Google and Amazon think big and they think bold. The other end of the spectrum is BlackBerry, J.C. Penney, and Radio Shack. Thinking bold, and using bold as a nomenclature (Blackberry Bold), are not the same thing.

Turnarounds and the Big Play

Nothing seasons a young manager like a turnaround. Reversing a weak business that is in red ink is an extremely painful process. It hardens you. And if you are fortunate enough to climb out of this pit of desolation, the principles and the culture that made the unthinkable possible become ingrained in you.

Figure 4.1 was introduced to me by Professor Nick Fry at an executive management program at the Ivy School of Business. It is a model I've followed ever since. The Crisis Curve: Urgency

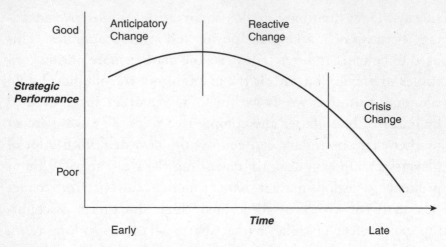

Figure 4.1 The Crisis Curve: Urgency for Action

for Action[4] applies to every business at every stage of its life cycle. Said another way, no matter where your company finds itself on the barometer of strategic strength, the curve categorizes the type of change that must be acted upon.

Here's how it works. Strategic Performance on the X Axis is measured by top-line indicators such as market share, sales growth trends, customer count, and brand image. The Y Axis of Time is divided into three segments described as Anticipatory Change, Reactive Change, and Crisis Change. Here are the business conditions that are present within each segment:

1. *Anticipatory Change.* Business is humming along nicely. Sales are up, customer demand is buoyant, market share and market size are increasing, and eager investors are keen to participate in your success. The early years of successful start-ups such as Chobani Yogurt and Warby Parker are a perfect fit for this time period. Why is this segment called "Anticipatory Change?" Because this is precisely the stage when a growth company needs to be thinking ahead, fixing the operation before it breaks, refreshing and revitalizing its strategic health. Warby Parker's recent decision to add flagship outlets to its online strategy is a great example

of anticipatory stage change-making. In most business domains, these strategic initiatives seem far from urgent. In the dynamic tech world, they are crucial.

2. *Reactive Change.* A sense of urgency begins to surface. Profits may be superb, but top-line growth is slowing or stagnating, and strategic health is weakening. This is where Campbell's and HP find themselves. Reactive change is the stage of the crisis curve that challenges "minding the store" types of leaders. These leaders find it difficult to institute transformational change when profitability is good. Shareholders in particular are blind to the fact that profitability can be the worse indicator of strategic health. At the outset, those who buy into change must still address two pertinent questions: what needs to change and where do we start?

3. *Crisis Change.* The urgency for action has never been greater. The company is strategically impaired and in need of reversal. Sales are in decline. Profitability has disappeared. Warehouses are full of aging inventory. Banks and suppliers are wary. Employees are depressed. Shareholders are panicking. People are jumping ship; headhunters are called upon to find "water walkers" for the C-suite. Four to five years ago, J. C. Penney and Blackberry were entrenched in the zone of Reactive Change. Today, they are full-fledged members of the crisis society.

At one time or another, I have traveled every inch of the crisis curve. Two technological innovations rescued Suchard's Canadian business from the extreme right of the curve and catapulted it to the far left. Novel vacuum-packing drove the sales line, and higher yield coffee roasting technology reduced costs of goods by 15 percent. Rather than take that entire savings to the bottom line, we shared it with the consumer, and brought prices down when quality and freshness were going up. Sales more than doubled. Margin increased by 50%, and profitability returned, for good—all from operating prudently within the doing less, better strategy. The incumbents didn't know what hit them. They'd thought we were dead.

Ten years after that turnaround, that same company was edging toward the curve of reactive change. When you near 30 percent of a large and lucrative market, top-line growth becomes challenging. I couldn't allow us to travel any further down that nasty slope. Once again, we would have to reinvent the company. We moved into the specialty coffee arena with more exotic blends and erected the only production facility in North America that would use only water to extract caffeine from green (unroasted) coffee beans. Now for the shocker—water decaffeination is by far the most expensive method of removing caffeine from coffee. We didn't care. Our Swiss Water Decaffeinated brand allowed us to add value to our own brand and to enter America's flourishing specialty coffee market. By the time Kraft bought the company, the majority of our Swiss Water Decaffeinated sales were to US specialty coffee retailers and roasters, including Starbucks.

Pretax earnings to sales within this specialty division of Jacobs Suchard were 30 percent—three times greater than the mainstream coffee we sold to grocery stores and mass merchandisers. Fundamentally, this was a backward integration strategy that allowed us to participate in the escalating gourmet coffee business as a niche supplier.

Follow me through our unique and profitable customer model for Starbucks. The starting point was contracting to decaffeinate Starbucks' coffee beans. Second, Starbucks-owned green coffee arrived directly from the producing country at our plant in 132-pound burlap bags. Except for country of origin identification, the bags were unmarked and unlabeled. Third, we emptied the coffee, decaffeinated it, and returned the decaffeinated beans to those bags. The step I adored was the fourth—we stenciled our "Swiss Water Decaffeinated" brand logo on the burlap and shipped the contents to Starbucks' roasting facility in Seattle.

Postsales service and marveling at the financials was the final step in the model. Our inventory cost: zero. Our fee for service: $1.00 per pound. The division's pretax profit per employee: $300,000.

Staying under the radar screen, creating a niche market, applying proven branded principles, and setting up an autonomous division with its own management team is how you go about earning 30 percent pretax profit on sales in the competitive food manufacturing sector. Was Kraft impressed with this when they acquired the company? Not in the least. They saw the Swiss Water Decaffeinated division as a nonconventional model—a poor fit and too small to worry about. They cared for supermarket channels. They still do. A few years after the acquisition, this business was spun off, and today the company continues as Ten Peaks Coffee with annual revenues of $60 million. I tip my hat to the entrepreneurs who acquired and added value to this excellent business. I'm told that Ten Peaks continues to decaffeinate coffee for Starbucks.

The first rule of a turnaround is freeing up the cash. The quickest means to this end is reducing inventory. Then you move on to selling off assets such as brands and equipment with a strategic end point in mind. If a piece of machinery moves, you paint it. If it doesn't move, you sell it. In the case of brands, it will be necessary to sever a limb to save a life—unloading a darling to preserve an entire enterprise. You have to work harder at doing less, better.

Make your first cut your deepest cut. This rule applies to divestments, business consolidation, and headcount reduction. You cannot set modest reduction goals; instead, slash your stock-keeping units, big time. To the old guard, the culling of the herd has to be seen as a bloodbath. If you reach for the stars, you won't end up with a handful of mud. As an example, assume you have made some aggressive cuts and managed to throw yourself a lifeline in newfound cash. That's not the end of it—far from it—you are still at the embryo stage of the reversal.

Ahead of you is a much more daunting task. You must find the ways and means to build strategic health into what remains of the fragile enterprise. Pull that off and you will have injected sustenance and sustainability into the rescue.

Sadly, most plans to improve sales and market share are based on spending more on advertising, introducing a battery of new products or line extensions, and expanding distribution. In a serious turnaround situation, these unadventurous, risk-averse measures never work. Conformist remedies increase the bleeding because they are not strategically transformational and game changing. One or two "big" plays make the difference.

The *Wall Street Journal* had this to say about Campbell's latest foray into soup renewal. "Campbell's is implementing more-efficient advertising and introducing tastier, more relevant products for today's consumer, like a new line of Slow Kettle soups with more-sophisticated flavors. The turnaround will take time."[5] No, the turnaround will not take time—the turnaround will not happen without transformational mind-sets at the top.

The Yahoo Play

When Yahoo CEO Marissa Mayer issued a ban on working from home, there weren't many supporters out there. Several journalists, tech pundits, and business leaders called her gambit regressive, old-school thinking, antifamily, and a giant step backward. However, none of the naysayers seemed to appreciate the magnitude of the turn-around situation she faced. Marissa was hired away from Google to reverse a four-year trend of eroding revenues. Yahoo was entering the "crisis mode" of strategic change. To fulfill any turnaround mandate, a leader has no choice but to initiate substantial cultural and strategic change with a firm hand, not a weak wrist.

Marissa is no stranger to the utopic corporate culture she is trying to create. She grew up in the house of Google, where employees were encouraged to come to work and work together to create magic. During her 13-year tenure, Google invested in making their facilities conducive to on-site collaboration. The strategy worked like a charm. Are these businesses or the factors for creating success that different? Why wouldn't she want this model for Yahoo? If the hordes of Yahoo's telecommuters were adding massive value to the organization, I doubt she would have risked their exit with this change in working conditions. I think she sized up the workforce and concluded that her most valuable employees were the ones prepared to come to work every day—the ones who would represent Yahoo's future.

Working from the office isn't for everyone, but let's be honest. There are a heck of a lot of folks out there who buy into the logic that working under one roof, side-by-side and face-to-face with colleagues, bolsters communication and collaboration. Ideas and insights come from personal interaction, whether those touch-points are in formal meetings or casual chats in hallways and cafeterias. When the heat is on to reignite a troubled business, it helps to have your colleagues close by. In times of need (particularly difficult turnarounds), the person in the next cubicle or across the table from you can be your emotional life support. "One Yahoo" means physically being together and moving in one direction like a flock of geese flying as a cohesive unit to a warmer destination.

Reversing several years of declining revenue hasn't been easy, and Marissa has a long way to go. Her first turn-around play was cultural. After a year, revenues and profits remain spongy, but Wall Street remains optimistic, with stock prices more than doubling since her appointment in 2012. To recapture the hearts and minds of current and future customers, her next play must accelerate the innovation pipeline and deliver relevant products and improved execution. In 24 to 36 months, Yahoo must be a different animal. Renewed competitive advantage lies in how Marissa's team fulfills her strategic vision. In her mind, everyone under one roof improves the odds of success. I'm in her corner, hoping she has chosen the right roommates.

The Hustle Approach

We are all familiar with the omnipresent on-stage presentations of the latest, greatest new technology gadgets. Business reporters love to cover these big-play stories. They were all over Facebook's initial public offering (IPO), their Instagram acquisition, and their announcement that their customer base had reached one billion users. Reports such as these helped drive Facebook's market share of the hundreds of daily business news posts. Google is another outstanding source of big stories. In 2008, journalists clamored to announce the launch of Google Street View, the digital facsimile of every street and laneway on the face of the earth. Not long after that came the news of Google Translate, an online translation service that did not require human translators. Today, Google Translate comes to you in 64 languages.

Should every company be striving for the form of strategic advantage that has become the hallmark of Amazon, Microsoft, Google, and Facebook? It's awfully hard to imagine surviving in the technology sector without it. Ditto other markets where technology advancement defines success or failure. There are all sorts of strategies that work in twenty-first-century business. At the top is the corporate strategy, followed by a smorgasbord of functional and subfunctional strategies ranging from foreign exchange to waste management.

Intense competitive rivalries were a fact of life in most of the businesses in which I was associated. But as you likely know, "poker stars" do not fuss over competitive rivalry the way "chessmen" do. The poker types are guided by the ethic of hustle. They sacrifice strategic navel-gazing and establish themselves as quick, nimble, paragons of tireless and flawless execution. These people get things done. That's one heck of an asset.

Hustle delivers superior results to thousands of retailers, restaurants, and service companies. I can't think of a better example than California-based In-N-Out Burger chain, ranked ninth as a great place to work in the United States by glassdoor.com, an online job and career community.[6] Unlike so many other fast food restaurants, this one delivers the "fast" in its nomenclature. In-N-Out Burger keeps it simple in order to deliver a great product, quickly. Their menu is pretty much limited to three beef burger offerings, fries, shakes, and soft drinks. If you want chicken, salad, pizza, or wraps, get out of the line to the counter and go elsewhere.

But In-N-Out is not strategically blind. I'm going to share a secret from the folks at In-N-Out that seems to contravene the do less, better mantra: "Urban myth or just plain excellent customer service? Ok, you've heard the rumors, wondered what was on it, maybe even felt a little left out of the loop. But in reality, we don't have any secrets at all. It's just the way some of our customers like their burgers prepared, and we're all about making our customers happy. So here are some of the most popular items on our not-so-secret menu.[7] In-N-Out then goes on to describe a few burger varieties that you won't see on the in-store menu board, including the 3x3, the 4x4, Animal Style, and Protein Style. Even with these variations for their best customers, haste, simplicity, and superior operational training allow this restaurant to do less, better, every time.

Equally nimble are some of the world's most successful private label brand manufacturers. Store brands, particularly in the United States appear to be doing better than ever. Nielsen reported a $111.6 billion mid-2012 running rate that was ahead of calendar 2009 sales by 18.5 percent.[8] Differing from In-N-Out Burger, which thrives on doing less, better, private label manufacturers prosper by doing more, better. They have to do more because the secret to success in this business is a wide array of products and packages in countless shapes, sizes, and flavors at costs substantially below branded competitors. This is just an entry chit into the private label industry.

Supremacy comes from the ability to satisfy America's large and powerful retail chains with flexibility, service, and predefined quality, all at the lowest price. This doesn't leave much room or time for these players to pioneer new technologies or develop their own brands. Most stay clear of proprietary branding; they are quite content to let the "branded" companies develop new products, new forms of packaging, and new manufacturing processes. Private label manufacturers aren't bashful about replicating competitive advancements. In fact, this is how they ensure that their retail customers are not disadvantaged. In rare cases in which "get it done" store brand makers pioneer innovations in systems, processes, products, or services, the innovations are seldom transformational. They are incremental, and easily copied. To the players in this game, that's not a big deal.

Hustle companies obsessively work at reducing costs and improving operations. They don't use their precious time to strategically hypothesize or intellectualize. They map a course of action and just do it. From top to bottom, everyone knows what is expected. Even recruiting is affected by the "get it done" strategy; these companies look for and hire hustlers.

These artists of action may be known for their ardent attention to the details of day-to-day activity, but don't for a minute think they lack farsightedness. Visions need not be so narrow that they suppress new ways of doing things. They must be broad enough that employees who thrive on perpetual motion can pursue and create wonderful new opportunities.

Strategic Naysayers

On the "hot seat" as a CEO, I constantly faced the pressing issues of bringing in the quarter, predicting commodity and foreign exchange markets, and responding to predatory competitive pricing. Suffice to say, most of the issues were short-term and operational rather than strategic. No matter what a company's product or service, these matters are not business anomalies. Whether the company is engaged in software, electronics, coffee, or fresh produce, squeaky wheels get the grease.

Luckily for me, I gained my stripes in strategic environments and learned how to balance operational challenges with strategic opportunities. Many senior managers haven't the foggiest idea how to do this—they are quasi leaders who can't differentiate between strategy and tactics. They want to leave their options open, and then unknowingly fall into a spiral of inconsistent decision-making and endless debate over solutions to nagging short-term problems. You can preach the value of narrowing market scope, reducing the product line, or cutting back stock-keeping units until the cows come home. They remain unconvinced.

I recognize that there are many people in leadership positions who desperately want to be more strategic. I also know that holding tough on strategy isn't always easy to do, especially when the heat is on. Those who go weak at the knees and lack the discipline to think strategically when it is most important to do so must dial up their intestinal fortitude. Ultimately, the less pressure one feels from day-to-day issues, the better the opportunity to think and act in the best long-term interest of the enterprise. Here are some ways in which leaders can deflect that pressure:

1. *Manage the Future.* This is at the heart of good strategic planning. Do not react to the future; rather, develop a path that gets you ready to define it. Now, get set and go.
2. *Be Proactive.* Follow the defined direction with daily actions that support the purpose. If strategic initiatives positively impact the market, competitors will react. Good. The greatest success comes from establishing new rules of the competitive game.

3. *Plan for Rainy Days.* An optional source of new revenue or a rainy day fund such as my "coupon reserve" can help off-set tough times that threaten to compromise the strategy. Caution: this is not strategic, but merely a short-term tactic to ease the pressure on profits.
4. *Manage Expectations.* Some folks call this sandbagging. I classify it is as prudent management. Set a stretch growth agenda, but make sure it is achievable.
5. *Accept the Fact That Sticking to Strategy Takes Courage.* Leaders without courage fold when the going gets tough.

In reference to point number 5, it was Peter Drucker who said, "Whenever you see a successful business, someone once made a courageous decision."[9]

No Kidding: Corporate Strategy on a Single Page

Strategists and strategic planners read the same periodicals and have similar destinations in mind, but there is a difference between the two. At the outset, the planners are disadvantaged by the definition of their role. They are staffers, not line managers. Strategic planning positions exist in many companies. Strategic planning is also a lucrative business for consultants who earn their living by the clock. The ramification of this practice is obvious. Strategic planning consultants can spend weeks, sometimes months, assessing, discussing, assembling teams, and conducting SWOT (strengths, weaknesses, opportunities, threats) analyses. In a *do less, better* world, SWOT should be pluralized. Adding the letter "S" to the acronym would force everyone involved in strategic planning into considering the sacrifices that should be made to strengthen the plan. A few pointed questions such as "How is that activity adding value?" or "What would happen if we stopped doing that?" might raise a few eyebrows, stir the senses, and bring strategic change.

Rather than break new ground, the strategic planning process led by consultants and strategic planners is usually a tortuous journey that concludes with a replication of the existing strategy. This is a complete waste of time. Crown corporations and government agencies are the worst offenders. I know a few things about crown corporations—for several years, I served as a director for the $3 billion British Columbia Lottery Corporation. The most recent strategic plans prepared by the largest crowns in British Columbia exceed 30 pages. In this age of transparency, these elaborate documents are posted online as "Service Plans," and they differ little from the versions of prior years. Strategic planners work on the construction. Take it from me. They are better bureaucrats than they are strategists; they do not make strategic sacrifice, and they do not do less, better.

A company's best strategists ought to dwell in the C-suite, with the CEO as the catalyst. I know this proclamation reeks of blasphemy to proponents and practitioners of the twenty-first-century flat organization. But the truth is that the company's most senior leaders—those who have their fingers on the pulse of the business and the industry—are best equipped to draft an effective strategic plan in a matter of days. The most prudent of strategists can bring clarity and purpose to a document within the confines of a single piece of paper.

So what's the difference between a one-page and a thirty-page strategic plan? The answers lie in the mind of the strategist.

Firstly, strategists are not obsessed with preparing beautiful documents for the purpose of public relations. Their obsession lies in bolstering their company's competitive advantage for the long term. Secondly, strategists are adamant about cutting through complexity, accepting (and sometimes seeking) sacrifice, and ensuring their plan is simple and clear. Thirdly, they motivate employees to invest substantial time and energy in the stated direction, unlike strategic planners, who collaborate with management to unearth strategic direction. Most importantly, strategists take the enterprise to the next level. For good reason, you won't find strategic planning departments at Twitter, Google, or Facebook.

That is the *why*. Now for the *way*. The foundation of every medium-term strategic plan should be deep strategic thought and the right conviction. The senior folks charged with preparing the plan must enter the process fully aware that this is not the annual budget; rather, it is the break from day-to-day operations—it represents the organization's future. By intention, the one-pager doesn't give the architect(s) much real estate to work with, even with the smallest of fonts. Include the content that matters—the well-articulated strategies, the initiatives, and the projects that will be critical in taking the company onward and upward.

Here is a blueprint for companies, business units, or divisions:

1. On a landscape page layout, establish your mission and/or vision at the top. If your company has both a mission and a vision, a sentence for each will suffice. This becomes your guide for defining the strategies necessary to achieving the goals.

2. Now draw a line down the middle of the page to create two sections. On the left is your Financial History and Outlook. Quantify two years of history, your best estimate for the current fiscal, and your three-year outlook. For these six years, enter sales, costs, margins, income, and key financial ratios, such as return on investment, return on assets, and return on sales—whatever is meaningful to management and the board.

3. On the right half of the page, below the six fiscal headings, are your Key Business Indicators (KBIs). The KBIs are those factors that determine your performance against the vision and/or mission—the factors that make your business tick. A company with differentiated branded consumables would likely measure market share, brand awareness,

brand image, and margin development. A service company would want to look at customer service, on-time delivery, out-of-stocks, and customer satisfaction levels. Low-cost producers like to stay abreast of costs, productivity, sales per employee, and overall employment. Some firms track new product launches, and some measure staff engagement. No matter the company, top management is responsible for increasing shareholder value. Quantify it. If your company is not public, look at the industry multiples of public companies and decide on a ratio in conjunction with your board of directors. Set your objectives annually and check your progress over the term of the plan.

4. Culture and Credo can be stated below the vision or after the quantitative section. Limit this to four or five existing traits and/or articulate the cultural goals that will inspire and engage the company's human resources. For example, you may say, "We strive to become more focused on fewer, bigger ideas so that we are swift and agile, proactive rather than reactive. 'Simplify and Go' is the modus operandi."

5. Finish up with the Key Strategic Initiatives. This is where the proverbial rubber hits the road—this is the stuff that drives the enterprise ahead. I like to limit the initiatives to no more than six or seven, and I try to represent each department. However, this is not always prudent, depending on the environment and the unique needs of the organization.

Once you have a draft of your medium-term plan, share it with your employees. Explain what you want to do, why it is important that it be achieved, and why you can't make it happen without their help. Ask for their input, make adjustments as necessary, and keep the final plan handy. That's the easy part. After all, it is only a single sheet of paper. Monitor progress and enjoy the journey toward the vision.

Oh, and one more thing...during my term as a director of that $3 billion lottery, I made sure that a one-page strategic plan guided that corporation. Top management and the board set the strategic direction for that plan. The strategic planning department took charge of the other plan—the 30+ pager that was published for the benefit of the public, the civil service bureaucrats, and the governing political party. That one was filed away, never again to be looked at by management until 12 months later.

Chapter 4 Summary

- Competitive situations shape distinct individual and team behaviors.
- Don't be blinded by the market share mentality. Think new markets, but make sure your entry is consistent with your core competencies and your strategic domain.
- There's not a better illustration to push corporate leaders into action than the "crisis curve." Every business enterprise can be found somewhere along that curve.
- Big game-changing plays are the remedies for companies in big trouble.
- Sick or healthy, if you keep doing what you've always done, the most you will get is what you already have . . . probably less. This is never the means to long-term business prosperity.
- Hustle is an underrated but very effective strategy for thousands of companies.
- Whether you are a start-up or a P&G, the ethic of focusing on what you do best and excelling at it is the culture and the identity that can sustain an organization's success for decades.

CHAPTER 5

Think Like an Entrepreneur

The previous chapters were concerned with the "less" of "do less, better." Now I'm going to swing the emphasis to the "better" part of the expression. Such discussions could cover a lot of ground. You won't get that from me. I'll keep it simple and focus on the betterment that can be found in entrepreneurial thought, brand marketing, and human capital.

Earlier, I implied that a good leader can cost as much as a bad one. I should have said that bad leaders actually cost more than good ones when you consider their negative impact on the enterprise and the hefty severance packages required to get them out. Good leaders inspire people to make the extra effort. The avenues they open in order to achieve superior business performance do not always have to cost money. Ingenuity and creativity can be as potent a resource to a Fortune 500 CEO as a panhandler.

Creating the right culture takes time, but once companies have it, and once people exercise it, the impact ripples through the organization all the way to the customer and the last line of the income statement. Culture is a state of mind—it is the things that really matter in the organization. Some organizations thrive on low-cost operations. Others pride themselves on moving fast and getting things done. Online retailer Zappos and environmentally conscious Patagonia are in a cultural league of their own. Culture IS the brand at these companies. When you have that, everything clicks.

Whining about the economy, budget constraints, and low-cost competition does nothing to improve the well-being of a business. Unleash your vision, your creativity, and your passion.

And while you are at it, don't forget to enjoy your journey. When you ride off into the sunset and join me in the corporate after-life, you will appreciate that the journey was worth more than the destination.

The Small-Business Ethic

In 1995, Hamdi Ulukaya knew a few words of English. Today, 1,300 people are churning out Chobani Yogurt from the once-shuttered plant he bought from Kraft. How did a small, New York yogurt maker with a dream break into a market domi-nated by Danone and Yoplait? It sure wasn't from a fat bank account. On the contrary, Ulukaya needed a US Small Business Administration (SBA) loan to buy the plant and fund commer-cial production.

Here is a business that continues to hire, while many other consumer goods organizations reduce staff. In an interview with *Entrepreneur Magazine*, Ulukaya said, "I can only speak from what happened to us here. I look at this plant in New Berlin. It formerly operated in almost the same industry and it was closed. What was wrong before? For me, it proves the need for small businesses. Every small business will give you an entrepre-neurial way of looking at things. I guarantee you that for every plant that closes, if you gave it to one small-business person in that community, he or she would find a way to make it work. The small-business attitude is you always find a way to make it work."[1] This assertion by an entrepreneur with a tendency to understate his own role in the Chobani's triumph is pertinent to every David and Goliath story.

Attitude costs nothing. Word of mouth is free. Social media is chicken feed compared to the expense of traditional broadcast media. A better product in consumer categories can cost a few more pennies to make, but with the right marketing proposi-tion and the right service ethic, that premium can be covered by a higher selling price. In the case of Suchard's triangular Toblerone Swiss chocolate bar, the production and packaging cost will be around 25 percent more than a Hershey bar, but that combination of Swiss chocolate, honey, and almond nougat will sell for more than double the price of most mainstream chocolate bars.

The intertwining of the low- to no-cost factors explains the evangelical loyalty bestowed upon Chobani. Although Danone has fought back in the Greek yogurt category and chipped away at Chobani's market share by relying on its big-company clout to squeeze prices, Chobani remains atop the exploding category with an estimated 39 percent of the segment and 18 percent of the total US market.

Bringing the Chobani dream to fruition was not without the usual start-up headaches that keep entrepreneurs awake at night. "It was lonely days, difficult days, a lot of question marks, a lot of pressure to see if I would make it to the next day,"[2] said Ulukaya of the early months. By their very enterprising nature, entrepreneurs struggle with the concept of focus. They see opportunity everywhere and possess an intrinsic desire to chase it down, bag it, and wrap it with a gold ribbon. By contrast, in the *Rock Center* interview with Harry Smith, Ulukaya cites his own focus and personal attention to five doctrines when explaining his company's success.

1. *Keep your product simple.* Know what you do and do it better than anybody else.
2. *Invest in your core*—For Ulukaya, that's the production facility. Capital investments of $193 million validate his belief that brick and mortar is the backbone of what Chobani does well. This leader invests in plant and equipment because he wants to. Most CEOs make these kinds of investments because they have to, and if the capital investment isn't urgent, they will put it off until next year or

the year after that. This is another difference between the builder's and the banker's state of mind.

3. *Market your products and your business with sincerity.* This is precisely the strategy for social media effectiveness. It is no surprise that Chobani is at the forefront of this medium. Is marketing with authenticity a sacrifice? Not to this entrepreneur.

4. *Watch the pennies.* Ulukaya runs his business with the mentality of a corner store proprietor. Cash is the driver. Lately, he has freed up a chunk of it to defend against Danone's aggressive price reductions. Beyond that, Olympic sponsorship and advertising during the 2014 games doesn't come cheap.

5. *Lead by example.* "If you make yogurt, go to the plant," he says. "Work with your people; if you want people to work on Sunday, be there next to them." For Ulukaya, that's a small sacrifice. For 50-year-old Ivy League CEOs, that notion is a million miles from their radar screen.

Interestingly, these tenets describe the habits of many successful entrepreneurs. Do you think the chief executives of Yoplait and Danone operate this way? If they did, they might have avoided the embarrassment of an immigrant farmer rubbing their corporate noses in yogurt cultures. Might this humiliation explain why Danone has roared back with price cuts rather than strategic smarts?

Can You See the Unseen?

Ulukaya saw the unseen. Some people consider that sense a gift from God bestowed upon the chosen few. Sports enthusiasts know of it from our greatest athletes. National Hockey League Hall of Fame player Wayne Gretzky had a knack for skating where the puck would be. He was equally proficient at passing the puck to a place where a teammate would be. Larry Bird moved a split second ahead of a National Basketball Association opponent's ball toss to make the steal. Joe Montana miraculously calculated the movements of everyone on the football field. Somehow, these superstar athletes saw the play before it happened.

Seeing the play before it happens is no longer overlooked as a key factor for entrepreneurial success. The business world boasts such notables as Mark Zuckerberg, Martha Stewart, Bill Gates, and Oprah Winfrey. Did any of these luminaries lose their sense of vision once they created their billion-dollar enterprises? Not in the least. Their hopes and dreams magnified. Steve Jobs believed in his ability to know what people wanted before they did. There was no point in asking; he knew consumers would love the iPod, the iPhone, and the iPad.

With these successes well publicized, you'd think every major corporation would encourage its leaders to embrace a similar philosophy. The constraint is the fear of failure and the inability to sacrifice risk-averse management paradigms. Marketing teams tirelessly research everything to death. Hiding behind the "consumer is boss" facade, these wimps who think of themselves as professional Brand Managers won't make the daring call without asking their customers for permission. Yes, the customer holds all the cards in the new world of social media, but marketers are the ones who shuffle the deck and deal those cards. In the deck of the best marketers, the Ace stands for beneficial products and services, the King is superb customer service, the Queen is collaboration, the Jack is ongoing, compelling solutions...and the deuce is the selling price.

If Howard Shultz had based the Starbucks vision on a blind taste test pitting his dark-roasted, full-bodied coffee against the milder, middle-of-the-road Folgers or Maxwell House, there would not be a $15 billion business employing 150,000 people around the world.

"Those who like us, will like us a lot" is how I'd paraphrase Howard's mantra. Twenty-five years ago, he made that clear as he drove me around Seattle, showcasing several of his outlets. In the years to follow, Starbucks became a giant, and Howard gave in to the lure of more sales from those who prefer mild flavors and an instant coffee. Not that long ago, Starbucks introduced Via Ready Brew and Blonde Roast coffees, the latter described as subtle, soft, and mellow. Howard had walked away from the brand's core product positioning. Starbucks was built, in part, by sacrificing the segment of coffee drinkers who enjoyed mild-tasting coffee. That conscious sacrifice strengthened the brand and facilitated superpremium pricing.

Henry Ford once said that if he would have asked people what they wanted, they would have opted for faster horses. See the unseen. Have the courage to give your customers what they didn't know they wanted. To do that, you will have to make some sacrifices, maybe even cull some of the herd. The better you know your business, the more comfortable you will be operating this way. You can chalk up that advice as another feather in the cap of the specialist.

When and Where Magic Happens

For decades now, giant corporations have been gobbling up competitors and dominating markets. In the process, they have suffered erosion of their competitive edge because those at the top struggled with rapid change. Innovation waned and stagnation set in. "Cutting the fat" shored up short-term earnings, but this is never the way to restore a company's strategic vigor.

Some of these giants embarked on reinventing themselves by simplifying decision-making and acting with haste. Innovation and entrepreneurial thinking began a comeback. But the world does not stand still for reinvention. During this cultural shift, systematic innovators, the likes of Trader Joe's, FedEx, and

Whole Foods, extended their leadership over the sleeping old guard.

The spark that ignites innovation or an entrepreneurial thought can be found within a magic circle that is miles from your comfort zone. Many of the individuals who pioneered the new economy and the information age saw their destination before they boarded their jet to the future. But once the execution of their vision was rewarded with explosive sales and stratospheric market value in the Promised Land, they never allowed themselves to fall into the badlands of complacency. Sadly, those who dwell in complacency will never arrive in the magic zone of innovation.

Magic never happens in cultures that don't idolize innovation. Institutionalizing innovation is a process. Leaders promote creativity and teamwork, as well as the procedures and systems that nurture the concepts that pump blood into their darlings. It is now in vogue to talk about innovation in annual reports, press releases, and mission statements. Hundreds of companies do this, but their idea of innovation is not the Google or Amazon idea of innovation.

Reflect on innovation within your organization. How many of the eight traits listed below are apparent? If your answer is "not many," then your CEO, or his or her successor has a whack of work to do.

1. *Inaction is frowned upon throughout the organization.* Innovators don't put ideas before scads of committees or tolerate moaning about inadequate resources such as staffing, data, or financing.
2. *"Ready, Fire, Aim" is the company mantra.* I'm not suggesting that you bet the farm on a big idea, nor did Tom Peters when he propagated this phrase. If the innovation has break-through potential, give it a shot now, in a "measured bite," rather than waiting months for all the information

that might reduce the risk. It is the "doing" that reduces risk by validating, altering, improving, or killing the original premise.

3. *Failure is lauded.* This may be an overstatement, but I'm trying to instill in you an important principle. Acceptance of failure may be a more realistic assertion. Leaders who take pride in giving novel initiatives a try, find the magic zone. These are typical queries from this type of leader: What did you learn along the way? How will you make it better next time? When will that be? Where and what should we sacrifice? And by the way, how can I help you?

4. *Every innovation is applauded.* Celebrations are held for anyone who has found a better way to get the job done. That includes receptionists, loading dock workers, and payroll clerks. Celebrations can come in a number of ways. I like the personal touch in the company of others. Because of overusage, text messages and emails can limit the impact. The legendary monthly newsletter still packs a punch, but an assembly of employees and a personal tribute? Golden.

5. *Successful innovations become corporate folklore.* We know this goes on at Apple, Walmart, Nike, and Disney—employees at these enterprises are still talking about Woz and Steve, Sam, Phil, and Walt. There isn't a better way to impress potential hires and motivate coworkers than telling or repeating stories of how Max, Suzy, Chris, and Marion came up with that terrific idea that...

6. *The company's leaders have track records of innovation success.* These are the people who stimulate innovation and permeate the culture throughout every nook and cranny of the organization. CEOs such as Richard Branson, Jeff Bezos, and Tony Hsieh get the press and the credit, but below them is an armory of innovators whose ideas make companies hum.

7. *The organization reeks of pride.* Historical photos, and success stories can be found in offices, reception areas, newsletters, websites, and social networks. For the most ardent employee or customer, the tattoo phenomenon gives license to permanently etch the logos or slogans of the company upon their skin. Imagine the power of the brands that are advertised for life in this medium. Harley-Davidson, Nike, and Disney's characters head the list.

8. *The company's strategic constraints are clearly defined.* Nothing is more demotivating for an innovator than to be told that the idea is great, but "off strategy." Leaders must define their strategic scope, and from there, set the talent of their team in motion.

There are times when you don't have to dig for innovation. Sometimes creativity and innovation consists of turning up what is already there. You don't need endless research studies and weeks of focus groups to unearth the insight that provides the spark for innovation. The idea could be a Eureka moment when a toothpaste brand manager notices that the orifice of his brand is 7 percent smaller than the market norm. Everyone knows that toothpaste is dispensed by length on the brush. Is there any reason why consumption would not improve if the orifice of that tube were enlarged? I was that brand manager, and although that happened a long time ago, don't go thinking these opportunities aren't out there waiting to be discovered in today's world of business. Such examples are showing up all the time on the popular American television show *Shark Tank*.

Until the digital age, innovation was the way of the entrepreneur. Big business wasn't expected to revolutionize because the giant's power, expressed by market value or balance sheet, gave them a ticket to pass Go. From that vantage point, acquiring, beating smaller players into submission, and expanding geographically made advancements on the game board so much easier. Now, this is the way of the horse and buggy. As industries continue to consolidate, the opportunity for new players, such as Chobani Greek Yogurt and Amy's Kitchen (organic foods), will increase the pressure on the behemoths to stop minding the same old stores and start opening radically different stores that thrill customers.

Entrepreneurial Corporations: Oxymoron?

So, where and how does a bright young talent land a job in one of these radically different stores? A couple of years ago, a business professor friend invited me to address a luncheon for students enrolled in his class on entrepreneurship. I told him that his students might be better served by the wisdom of a social media whiz kid or techie half my age.

He countered with, "They've already heard from those guys. I want you for the balance. They need a perspective on innovation and entrepreneurship within the corporation—if that exists."

I accepted the task, assuming his students believed corporate management and entrepreneurship were principles of contradiction. The contrarians were likely members of the flat earth society. I decided to tackle the assumption head-on by addressing the culture of corporate Goliaths—the institutions responsible for creating the preconception. I referred to the brain-and-muscle concept that I wrote about earlier, as well as the challenge of real innovation among the old guard. No matter the size of the organization, we have bureaucratic companies, entrepreneurial companies, and plenty in-between. "In the race to the future, there will be drivers, passengers, and road kill."[3] Innovators drive the new marketplace, passengers watch it grow and eventually join in, and those who miss the revolution entirely are road kill. Kodak is road kill. They missed the digital photography revolution that nullified their film-based business model. The sad irony for this iconic company is that a Kodak engineer invented the first digital camera.

My friend's students saw themselves as entrepreneurial thinkers, yet at graduation, most of them will walk a path to the corporation. Some will use the experience as a springboard to entrepreneurial ventures. The rest will be "lifers." Their eyes widened when I smacked them across the forehead with that two-by-four of reality.

"Don't worry," I quickly added, "corporate life doesn't have to be a death sentence. Choose a company with a buoyant culture and a management that's not afraid of change. The change-makers are small to medium-size enterprises that thrive within niche categories, create new categories, or are keen to knock the big guy from the top rung of a mass market ladder. That's where you'll find entrepreneurial thinking."

Their eyes told me they needed more, and I was prepared to give it. To students who see themselves as "entrepreneurs in waiting" and are eager to begin their business careers in the right corporate environment, I recommend these search criteria:

1. *Seek out the small player or a division of a large player in a category you like.* At 9,000+ employees, Electronic Arts (EA) is big, but it is broken down into 40 innovative operations around the world. In 2012, EA showed its first profit in five years, albeit only $76 million on turnover of $4 billion. That modest profit edged up in 2013 to $98 million.[4] Sure, EA is watching their pennies; a cut in the number of operations would be a quick fix for most companies of this magnitude. I'm thinking that EA resists mass consolidation because they do not want to stifle innovation, a critical success factor in the video game business in which they have the lion's share.

2. *Pick an industry on a high growth curve.* The leaders of these companies are the ones who believe innovation is their

status quo, their business as usual. With the exception of smaller companies that have found unique niches, the conventional consumer packaged goods industry has lost its luster. Social media, telecommunications, and high tech are today's rising stars.

3. *Read the company's mission/vision statement.* Is it clear? Is it focused? Does it excite? Does it tell you what the company does for its customers and why its employees will want to go the extra mile to close in on the vision? The acid test is to ask the front-line employee what the company is all about and see if the response mirrors the mission.

4. *Know the reputation of the CEO and the other C-suite executives.* This isn't difficult to ascertain. The style of the company often reflects the values of the CEO, provided that person has been in the job for several years. The CEO of Mondelez is a lawyer who came up through Kraft's legal department. I've never met Irene Rosenfeld, but I'd be shocked if she were a risk taker. In all likelihood, she does a superb job managing risk, but there is little chance she will act entrepreneurially or champion the tenets of entrepreneurship.

5. *Beware the entrepreneur.* Given my views on Hamdi Ulukaya and several other entrepreneurs whom I admire, this opinion may set you back a step. Consider the fact that the autocratic Donald Trump is also an entrepreneur. He calls the shots, and his people execute. If you work in one of his companies, I suspect you will not operate entrepreneurially or learn the lessons of successful entrepreneurship. Don't overlook the entrepreneurs. Just be sure to research your target and proceed with caution.

6. *Explore companies that promote diversity.* Teams composed of individuals with different backgrounds generally find faster, better ways to solve problems. In diversity there is unity. Check the market cap of the world's leading companies in diversity. There's a connection.

7. *Don't resist entry-level jobs.* Upon graduation, I wanted to work in brand management or advertising. A seasoned pro at an advertising agency told me the way to do this was to take a job in the sales department. I joined Bristol Myers, managed a territory, and made local decisions—albeit on a very small scale. Within two years, I was in brand management.

8. *Position your inexperience as a competitive advantage.* Another surprising assertion? Not necessarily. I look at people entering the workforce as the fruitful new generation. If this is you, I suggest you take an approach something like this: "I'm eager to learn, keen to grow and hell-bent on making a contribution. I'm not stuck in a paradigm. And most important...I'll not rest until I find a workplace passionate about creativity and innovation." If an employer doesn't value this attitudinal competitive advantage, scratch them from your list. One day they will come a-calling; they'll need an entrepreneurial thinker to pull them out of their self-inflicted mess.

Innovation and the Under-40 Crowd

The organizations that make up Fast Company's annual list of the World's 50 Most Innovative Companies are the businesses whose products and services are having an enormous impact across their industries and our culture. Ninety percent of these organizations have yet to experience a midlife crisis because they haven't reached the age of 40. Are we to deduce that the new economy and early-stage life cycle businesses have a stranglehold on innovation and entrepreneurship? The evidence may lead one to draw that conclusion, but this does not have to be the case.

Fast Company's 2012 list included Siemens AG (founded 1847) and UPS (founded 1907). In 2013, Coca Cola (1886),

Ford (1903), and Corning (1851) joined the esteemed league, and in 2014, GE (1892) and Levi Strauss (1853) were recognized as outstanding innovators. These seven organizations that have reinvented themselves are proof that old economy companies can rise from the ashes of inertia or remain vibrant. P&G, an $80 billion consumer products company that has done business for 178 years, continues to change with the times. I'm on record as criticizing big companies for being slow, risk averse, and boring. However, like every rule, there are exceptions. Walmart, Microsoft, Oracle, eBay, Amazon, and Google are mega-billion dollar companies that have proven over and over again that they know how to sustain innovative cultures. If the leadership attitude is conducive to innovation, size does not matter.

Looking down from the CEO afterlife, I see so many examples of old economy CEOs who do not know how to revolutionize, fear the risks that come with true innovation, or simply do not comprehend the proper definition of the word. If decline or stagnation isn't already tormenting the dinosaur organizations they lead, it soon will. Innovation is the only catalyst I know that will generate organic growth out of years of malaise. What should be done to rectify this problem?

If I were an influential shareholder of one of these organizations, I'd begin, not by mandating that my CEO get busy creating an environment conducive to transformational change, but by replacing that CEO. Incremental improvement isn't a remedy for strategic ill health. Leaders who have thrived within innovative environments have the right stuff; these individuals demand revolutionary measures, and they are prepared to make the necessary sacrifices to achieve it.

Zig and Zag Energy

Sometimes, the idea that sparks the innovation will come easily—sometimes the idea is already past the embryo stage in the visionary's mind. The energy drink phenomenon is one such idea.

In the mid-'80s, former Jacobs Suchard marketer Dietrich Mateschitz found his inspiration on a trip to Thailand, where he discovered a local energy drink called Krating Daeng. Mateschitz was intrigued by the English translation (Red Bull), and with a Thai partner, he went about refining the product's concept and modifying the ingredients to suit Western tastes. In 1987, Mateschitz's version hit the shelves in Austria.

Mateschitz was not chasing market share—the energy drink market did not exist. But he had seen the unseen; he believed he could create the market. You see, Mateschitz understood the power of brand image. He grew up in the marketing departments of the European consumer packaged goods industry. Unlike any other food or beverage brand, Red Bull's image would be irreverent and rebellious as expressed by the when, where, why, and how of its consumption. This thinking was exceedingly entrepreneurial for a blue-chip packaged goods marketer of that day and age. Of course, Mateschitz was not your typical blue-chip packaged goods marketer.

He began his entrepreneurial quest by targeting the college crowd. Devoid of a budget anywhere close to what he had on Jacobs Coffee, Mateschitz relied on sampling, and he was remarkably successful in achieving word-of-mouth awareness. For more than 25 years now, Red Bull has tenaciously abided by the founder's strategic vision in everything it does. The brand's differentiation is its "cult" imagery and the "buzz" created by break-through marketing executions that continue to embed its distinctive reputation. As sales grew, Mateschitz leveraged the growth and invested in sports and entertainment events, sponsored by Red Bull and directed at young urban professionals. He never looked back, even though he had a band of predators chomping at his heels. Global sales from a 165 countries topped $6 billion in 2012.[5]

The current slogans, "Red Bull Gives You Wings" and "No Red Bull, No Wings," are as strategic as you can get. Their message relates not only to the stimulating properties of the product but also the way Red Bull's customers want to live their lives. For this emotional benefit, users gladly sacrifice their dollars for a super premium price. Red Bull's brand strategy is tight, but its culture is freewheeling, affording each country the liberty to pursue event strategies that fit the marketplace. To this end, in Canada, Red Bull is music and arts centric, owning gallery space to exhibit quirky and nontraditional art such as Canada's Best Doodle Art.[6]

This company is obsessed with revolutionary thought, especially in publicity and promotion. A few years ago, they realized they were becoming one of the biggest content sources of action sports and culture on the planet. So they created a revenue-generating media entity that produces content wherever followers of the Red Bull lifestyle might be. The content of Red Bull Media House is pervasive in the digital media world. Beyond action sports, this amazing company is pushing the limits of programming and producing content of interest to its potential audience, such as the documentaries *Red Bull Street Kings* (the power of hip-hop to improve the lives of Ugandan children), *The Art of Flight* (a standout snowboarding film), and the mind-blowing *Mission to the Edge of Space* (to advance scientific discoveries for the benefit of mankind).

Insiders seem to think that revenues from the media division will eventually exceed those of the energy drink. Check out the Red Bull Stratos website and ask yourself whether Pepsi or Coke would ever think of such game-changing stuff. Coke may be innovative, but the harsh reality is that the Cokes and Pepsis of the world have realized that their conventional and cultural mind-set isn't suited to the rebellious cult brand arena. Both have given the energy segment a good try, but with marginal success, at best. Giants struggling to enact entrepreneurial and creative cultures ought to avoid getting drawn into wars they cannot win.

Red Bull's greatest challenge in the marketplace has actually come from another entrepreneurial company, the Monster Beverage Corporation. If Red Bull is the strategically disciplined "zig" of the energy drink business, Monster Energy is the disorderly "zag." Monster does a marvelous job of contradicting the tenets of strategic sacrifice and focus. I include this company in the book to point out that there are exceptions to every rule, and in Monster, we have the quintessential example.

The Monster Beverage Corporation has been around since 2002. In 2013, it delivered sales of $2.3 billion and earned $340 million after tax.[7] For a company that's breaking the golden rules of business strategy, $340 million is a gigantic return. There must be good reason for this.

Like Dietrich Mateschitz, the entrepreneurs behind Monster started with an idea—a cool brand name, an intrusive logo, and the determination to create a defiant brand image. The brand was positioned as the anti-cult to the market leader. When your brand attains cult status (both Monster and Red Bull enjoy this imagery), you have power. Monster has exercised that power without suffering punitive damage. Here is a summary of the golden rules as they apply to the behaviors of zig and zag:

Be first in. Every strategist appreciates the "early bird gets the worm" theory. Red Bull's dominant market share and staggering sales and profits should be proof enough. Entrepreneurs also appreciate the rewards bestowed by preemptive action, but they aren't dissuaded by not being first in. In this quirky sector, the second mouse managed to take a healthy bite out of the cheese—in this case, the number two position in the mushrooming market.

If you can't be first in, make a better product. The energy drink category is not as much about product differentiation as it is about image and target group distinction. That's not to say a market follower can get away with launching inferior products.

It simply means that parity is workable when conspicuous consumer benefits on the emotional spectrum are relevant. This condition has existed in the US mainstream beer market for as long as I can remember. The morose beer market could use a good dose of energy, but more on that later.

Focus on one category and keep it simple. Zag takes the contrary view. I counted 20 subbrands in the portfolio and over a hundred stock-keeping units. On top of that, the Monster logo is pervasive—you see it on an array of items ranging from apparel to condoms—so much for sacrifice and doing less, better. So much for the principles espoused in Al Ries and Jack Trout's best seller, *The 22 Immutable Laws of Marketing.* Al and Jack devoted an entire chapter to urging brand marketers to avoid gratuitous line extensions.

Control your own distribution. Monster relies on third-party distributors to get their products on retailer shelves and into bars and taverns. This is the lowest cost way to introduce a beverage in the United States, but it sure isn't controlling one's distribution destiny. It is relying on several others. Yet, in an industry where distribution scale economies are a tremendous advantage, market reality trumps strategic theory.

Create economies of scale. Coca-Cola and PepsiCo have a long history of success with scale. Both companies' energy drink offerings (Coke's Full Throttle and Pepsi's AMP) benefit from manufacturing and distribution economies. But here, scale is not the secret to success with the consumer. Branding is. Even the clout and vast marketing muscle of Coke and Pepsi could not bolster market share of their brands beyond single digits. Scale has a nasty way of inflicting complacency into C-suites.

Never introduce a premium brand concept at a low price. Monster snubbed its nose at this tenet by launching 16-ounce cans at the same unit price as Red Bull's 8.3-ounce size. Discount prices seldom work in the long haul. So far, the strategy has worked wonders for zag.

Despite Monster's success, do not try to emulate their business practices, but rather look to zig as the model for success.

In Red Bull and Monster, we have two similar products, two strategic paths, and two highly successful enterprises that zig and zag to economic prosperity. But remember this: the one that followed the principles of strategic marketing with outstanding creativity and entrepreneurship remains the leader. For the long haul, I predict the divesture of Monster (likely to Coke, which recently took a 16.7% stake with an option for up to 25%[8]) and the widening of Red Bull's leadership, no matter who acquires number two.

The "Going Green" Sacrifice

There's not likely to be a responsible CEO who hasn't pondered how to make his or her business more sustainable. Whether a leader is driven by personal ethics, a socially changing world, headlines praising "sustainable" organizations, opportunism, or outright greed, business is finally responding to the green trend—albeit slower than many of us would like to see. And although the captains of industry may have the "will" to transform their companies, the "way" is continually blocked by inefficiencies, higher costs, and unacceptable returns on the investment in technology. To successfully pursue the green-paved highway, sacrifices will have to be made.

In the case of Houweling's Tomatoes, it happened to be a purely economic mandate that introduced the greenhouse farmer to the world of green business. To some, this may sound crassly capitalistic. Yet, when all was said and done, the end product of an entrepreneur's bottom-line incentive emerged as a world-class model of agricultural sustainability. Who can argue with that?

Casey Houweling had a big idea. He wanted to create a "semi-closed, over-pressured" tomato greenhouse designed for hot, arid climates that would recapture heat, generate solar energy, reuse every drop of water, and produce the most delicious tomatoes on the planet. Becoming the farm of the future did not come cheap. Casey invested $50 million into the project. This explains why competition is reluctant to catch up, and attests to the tenacity of this visionary.

If you tour the Camarillo, California, facility, you will find a four-acre man-made pond that captures rain water and run-off. Irrigated water that is not consumed by the tomato vines is filtered, treated, and reused, eliminating runoff that can pollute the water table. In addition, five acres of photovoltaic solar panels generate 1 megawatt of green electricity, equivalent to removing 6,400 cars from the road for a year. Houweling's latest innovation is the installation of three natural gas cogeneration engines. The first greenhouse application of its kind in America, Houweling's generates 13.2 MW of electricity, delivering excess power to the Southern California grid. Additionally, heat and CO_2, traditionally waste products of combustion, are captured and used for heat and fertilization to enhance plant growth.

While the project appears like a no-brainer, it required an incredible commitment by Houweling and his team to make it a reality. Faced with miles of red tape and reams of paperwork, the persistent entrepreneur stormed ahead and got the job done.

"While it hasn't been easy," he said. "Today we are operating a 13.2 MW installation that significantly reduces our environmental impact, while increasing our ability to grow and harvest year-round, locally grown tomatoes. We made the decision to move forward with the first combined heat and power installation in a US greenhouse without the certainty of a power purchase agreement. It was a huge risk, but at the end of the day, I believe in this technology and know it was the right thing to do." Ah, the entrepreneurial spirit and green capitalism are alive and well.

Here is a medium-sized company enjoying a significant return on its invested capital and realizing additional benefits from a green strategy. Customers are taking notice. The Houweling's brand is expanding its distribution among grocers who value quality and sustainability. Employees take pride in their company's lead, and the corporate values are now firmly engrained in the tenets of green business.

Chapter 5 Summary

- You don't have to be an entrepreneur to think like one.
- Culture is a state of mind—innovation can't happen without an innovative culture.
- Innovation's Promised Land is miles from the comfort zone.
- Attitude costs nothing. Word of mouth is free. Creativity and ingenuity are the best bargains in business.
- "Fire, Ready, Aim" is the innovator's mantra.
- Social media has leveled the playing field for the little guy. But large or small, great ideas and flawless execution are the conduits for success.
- In the realm of business innovation, "seeing the unseen" is the difference between good and great.
- It is not the money, but the idea that drives entrepreneurship.

CHAPTER 6

KISS Is Not a Rock Band

Thirty years ago, I read Theodore Levitt's classic, *The Marketing Imagination*. In the book, the renowned marketing professor said there was no such thing as a commodity, only people who think like commodities. I stopped using the "C" word. So should you. Differentiation is still the name of the marketing game. Distinction in service, image, and promise allows a brand to occupy a piece of your busy mind. More importantly, it is that brand's raison d'être, its reason for being, that causes you to think of it when you are ready to shop. This is the brand that goes into your virtual shopping cart. Should you decide to edit your cart, the marketer is hopeful that you will increase the quantity before proceeding to checkout.

Notwithstanding this generally accepted principle, several big brand marketers, known as the fathers of brand management, have fallen on their own swords. Marketers of beauty aids, beverages, food, and soap became so hung up with image differentiation that they overlooked the inherent value of the product. Private labels picked up the slack. The differentiation focus within high-tech and new age companies is the product itself; once these companies carve out product distinction, they call on marketing for the sizzle that sells the steak. Then they walk the talk all the way from their shipping dock to post-sales and service. We live in a day and age where brilliant marketing can no longer "sell ice cubes to Eskimos." Yet, marketing is every bit as important today as it was 50 years ago.

If you want differentiation, you have to ask yourself this question: what am I prepared to sacrifice to get it? Differentiation in marketing requires giving up a benefit or two or three to make a compelling promise. In this chapter, KISS isn't a 1970s rock band. KISS is an acronym for "keep it simple, stupid." The drums of this long-serving, tried and true concept continue to beat in this complex world. Those who embrace the notion are the winners. Promising service is easy. Airlines, telecoms, and credit card companies promise customer satisfaction all the time. Do they deliver it?

One of my clients was the privately held Rich Corporation of Buffalo, New York. My assignment was to recommend some exciting new products for their SeaPak shrimp operation in St. Simons Island, Georgia. At the time, virtually all of SeaPak's seafood offerings were frozen breaded shrimp of one form or another. It became evident that some of SeaPak's management expected entries into other seafood categories. Extending the line didn't seem that much of a strategic jump.

To the contrary, with some help from culinary enthusiasts, I presented a dozen new product concepts—all shrimp—none battered or breaded, and every one of them differentiated, higher-end propositions. And, as you might guess, all were frozen, in line with SeaPak's competencies in production, sales, and distribution. SeaPak's management of the day liked what they saw, particularly the uniqueness of the concepts and the move to premium imagery and premium margins. I also convinced them to change the name of the company from "SeaPak" to "The SeaPak Shrimp Company" and use that nomenclature as the mother brand to hammer home shrimp specificity. This was a no-brainer because SeaPak's major shrimp competitors were broadline seafood companies like Gorton's, Van de Kamp (Pinnacle Foods), and High Liner.

Times change and so do managements. Today, this division of Rich's is known as "The SeaPak Shrimp *and* Seafood Company." The lineup now includes clam sticks, popcorn fish, tilapia tenders, crab cakes, and a couple of fish burgers. Did the world need another crab cake or another fish burger?

No. SeaPak's expanded lineup is readily available from others. Seemingly, someone had an idea to add this array of non-shrimp items to bolster the income statement. Presumably, in the name of consistency, "Seafood Company" was added to the branding. One assumes that these items would contribute significantly to SeaPak's sales and profit for management to sacrifice their positioning as a shrimp specialist. Not so. There was nothing that I could find from Rich's or SeaPak to indicate a product advantage or any sign of potent advertising or promotion to support this mishmash of nonstrategic, "me too" line extensions. This exercise was not a case of consumer insight, but rather an example of giving up glorious strategic differentiation for nothing more than added complexity and gratuitous sales. In the process, SeaPak has transformed itself from a marketer to a supplier.

In the high-tech and information age sectors, consumer and customer insight is the precursor to product and service differentiation. Successful companies don't stumble upon insight. Inquisitive marketers burrow for it and conceptualize it. Then they act upon it. That can mean redesigning the traditional marketing department to include an infrastructure for social media and a chief content officer position. Great marketing becomes the cultural glue that binds every department and every employee to the vision—always has, always will.

The Ultimate in Brand Management: Creating a Brand

Astute branding is the great equalizer in business. You know what Red Bull and Monster did with it—they successfully outmaneuvered two giants, Coke and Pepsi. Monster's brand positioning lived by the tenets of creative single-mindedness, and although they wandered strategically, it was their cult branding that allowed them to succeed without strategic adeptness.

Soon after its nineteenth-century conception, another giant became the world's quintessential marketing institution. Selected by Fortune as the world's ninth most admired company in 2012 and ranked fifteenth in 2013 and 2014, P&G's perennial performance as measured by growth in sales, profit, and shareholder value is outstanding. This company's arsenal includes a stable of brand leaders. At last count, 26 of them had surpassed $1 billion in annual sales. I'm venturing a guess that with 120,000 employees in 80 countries, P&G has churned out a hundred thousand brand marketers in its long existence. Here's the dirty little secret on P&G: 99 percent of those marketers have never created an entirely new brand from scratch. Allow that to sink in for a moment.

Brand Managers inherit brands and manage existing franchises much like their predecessors did. They may launch line extensions, new sizes, and different forms of packaging, but this doesn't count. Creating a new brand from a distinct concept, giving birth to the baby, naming it, promoting it, and watching it grow is the most fulfilling experience a marketer will ever realize. That doesn't happen very often within mega packaged goods companies. In the tech world it happens every day. The latest tablet is a hell of a lot more than a line extension. It has to be. If the upgrade doesn't possess distinguishable new product features that outperform its mother, father, or the competition, it is dead—and the marketer will know that within a matter of weeks.

For those marketers not engaged in tech, other new age markets, or start-ups, there is a way for you to give birth to a brand, but your reward for your little darling's prosperity will not be in the usual currency.

Organizations desperately in need of brand marketing expertise are charities. Yes, many are already well branded, such as Oxfam, World Wildlife Fund, and the United Way. But with each passing day, there are new foundations emerging for very good reason—local runs, walks, and rides for cancer, heart disease, hospices, hospitals, and medical research. These types of charities are organized by volunteers who generously give their time for causes in which they passionately believe. Despite the financial pressures facing America, more than $400 billion was donated to charitable agencies in 2013, an increase of 12.9 percent over 2012.[1] Ask any of them if the annual donations they take in are adequate. You know the answer.

For each charity to make its mark in an overcrowded marketplace, the organization must fight for a share of mind and a share of the humanitarian wallet. Just like a business brand, this is achieved by effectively communicating the organization's platform and making damn sure that platform doesn't violate the rules of KISS. Charities offer marvelous opportunities for marketers to volunteer their time to create and manage a brand that captures the vision, the values, and the beliefs of a worthy cause.

A few years ago my son, David, created such a brand on behalf of a young doctor who wanted to run across Canada to raise prostate cancer awareness among younger men. Dr. Riley Senft had lost a grandfather to prostate cancer, and his father was battling the same disease for the second time in five years. The statistics were eye-opening. In Canada, one in six men will be diagnosed with the disease. Riley's family history implied that his chances of being diagnosed with this type of cancer were more than double the norm. Despite those odds, current treatments post an amazing success rate of over 90 percent when detected early. So the run, in addition to raising funds and making younger men aware of the risks, was about encouraging the target group of 25- to 44-year-old males to seek early detection when certain conditions became present.

With that background, David went about defining this charity's brand positioning the way he would a commercial product. By carefully managing other eager volunteers who wanted a multitude of brand promises, he managed to stay the simplicity course defined by KISS and settle on this simple, clear, yet comprehensive brand strategy:

Brand Name:	Step into Action
Brand Benefit:	Saving the lives of prostate cancer's future victims
Reason to Believe:	Early detection is your first step
Brand Personality:	Serious, passionate, with a touch of irreverence
Brand Slogan:	"One finger can save your life"

There is nothing convoluted about the elements of this strategy; the simplicity ought to be the guide for any commercial product or service. But as you know, great strategy is useless without great execution. How was David going to bring attention to a cause that lacked a communications budget? The answer came from the best bargain in business—creativity. The call to action for this charitable endeavor was the rectal examination, and the provocative slogan, "One Finger Can Save Your Life" actually came to life when illustrated with an extended forefinger out of a fist that conjured up the image of the raised middle finger, universally recognized as an impolite gesture. Never more motivated, Riley pressed forward and ran from the Atlantic to the Pacific Ocean in 154 days, which included several stops along the way for more than 50 radio, television, and newspaper interviews. By the time he dipped his foot in the Pacific, he had jogged approximately 4,350 miles and raised $617,000 for prostate cancer research.

As for your opportunity to invent a brand, I suggest you step into action and put your marketing mind to a cause you care about. Use your strategic expertise to break through the message clutter with an identity that quickly conveys the charity's vision and values to the target audience. Imagine the satisfaction of seeing the results of your efforts. Your regular job need not stop you from convincing the public to fund a new hospital wing, feed the homeless, or provide accommodation for families of terminally ill children.

Marketing Management Performance Review

Every marketer worth his or her salt wants to build brand equity. Those who work in brand management for the more sophisticated consumer products organizations periodically check brand awareness and brand attributes to monitor progress. For a moment let us assume that the fictitious Hogwash Detergent is positioned as the brand that promises the whitest wash. Let's also say that 35 percent of adults in a 2014 usage and attitude study say that Hogwash Detergent is "best at getting clothes clean." That percentage needs to go up in two or three years to unequivocally validate an improvement in brand equity. Simple enough? Not quite. Consider this exchange between Hogwash Detergent's general manager (GM) and the brand's marketing manager whom I'll call Janet. Janet is trying to rescue a social media budget that the GM has earmarked for another project.

"Okay, Janet," says the GM, "you're telling me that the awareness and image of Hogwash is up by a couple of percentage points versus the last survey. If that's the case, why am I not seeing any growth in profit?"

Mindful that the impact of communication initiatives can take time, Janet says, "As you know, our brand-building effort is an investment in the future. In this challenging economy, we can't expect overnight results. Eventually, sales and profit will respond."

"Invest in the future is the line Bob fed me five years ago when he ran the brand. I'm still waiting for this future. When can I expect it to arrive?"

During this bout of sparring, both Janet and the GM scored some points. In the case of capital projects, every proposal includes a payout, and performance is always measured against the payout parameters. Investments in marketing campaigns generally avoid this type of prudent scrutiny. When this occurs, marketing accountability is also avoided. Having come up through the marketing function, I valued brand imagery enhancement, and as a CEO I appraised and remunerated for brand equity growth. To do this, it was critical that my CMO and I agreed on how enhanced brand equity impacted our business. To make it easy and keep it simple, we settled on statistical unit sales, market share, and margin. There are many ways to drive volume and profit within a fiscal year. Increased brand equity generally isn't one of them, but over the medium- and long term, it is the critical factor in bettering a brand's strategic health and enhancing the income statement. We measured and rewarded brand equity growth in the following ways.

1. We determined the sales/share/margin relationship and measured it annually. Assuming an absence of major uncontrollable factors such as crop failures, we believed that improved brand equity occurred when . . .
   a. sales were up and unit margin was flat or up versus the previous year,
   b. market share was up and margin was flat or up, and
   c. sales were flat and margin was up.

   As it applies to sales and margins, the unsavory outcomes were a) sales and margin down and b) sales flat/up and margin down. Reading between the lines, margin was the most important indicator of brand equity. This is characteristic of the premium brand marketer's mentality—prudent brand managers at Porsche, Grey Goose, Gucci, and Chanel understand this.

2. If Janet's Hogwash brand delivered any of the positive equity prerequisites, Janet was in for a hefty bonus. Sure, at Suchard, there were years when the numbers didn't move or the improvement was small, and correspondingly, the

bonus would also be small. But for those managers who stuck around and performed, the appreciation in dollars and cents was always there.

When Kraft rode over the moat and into our castle, I had the opportunity to directly compare the profit and loss statements of our coffee brands with those of our new shareholder. The difference in the numbers and the financial ratios brought a wide grin to my face. I sobered up when I considered where those brands and their equity would be headed. In a company the size of Kraft, manufacturing hundreds of products in dozens of categories, it is impossible for the most senior, most experienced people to give the majority of their time to one or two businesses. For management attention, local brands lose out to global brands every time, and that was the case with Nabob Coffee under Kraft.

The Church of Brand

Not long ago, L'Oréal celebrated its one hundredth birthday, and *Advertising Age* published an impressive tribute to this passionate marketing company. Over those 100 years, the L'Oréal moniker has become synonymous with the image of the classic Parisian—upscale, exclusive, and aspirational. Notwithstanding a few ethical missteps along the way, such as overexaggerated airbrushing,[2] L'Oréal has adeptly negotiated through time's minefields, setting the branding standard for the cosmetics industry.

Indeed, it makes sense that any industry whose cost of production is a single digit on the sales dollar knows how to add value. But to do it consistently well . . . to embed in the customer's mind the tangible and emotional values that garner outrageous prices over the long haul . . . well, the marketer must be an esteemed parishioner of the Church of Brand. L'Oréal's global brand competitors can also be found in the congregation—P&G, Unilever, Shiseido, and Estée Lauder round out the top five. In the social media arena, cosmetic and personal care products excel at something called "brand reference positivity," defined as brands that people talk about positively.

Is there any other industry that can compare to beauty care for perennial branding consistency and success? Some say beer marketers are savvy. Beer is certainly a fast-paced business in which advertising and branding are vitally important. But with the exception of Budweiser and a handful of upscale European brews, beer brands have not weathered the cruel test of time. Under pressure to deliver tonnage, beer marketers have surrendered message consistency in their quest for an uptick in market share. Campaigns come and go as fast as the advertising agencies that create them. Brand complexity enters the customer's mind. Confusion is the outcome.

The soft drink makers aren't much better, but they get away with communication inconsistency because the market is comprised of two big players. Notwithstanding the strategic accolades I have bestowed upon Coca-Cola, generations of Coke marketers have deployed 56 slogans over a century of advertising[3]—that's a new one every two years. Some of those catchphrases have been excellent. "The pause that refreshes" (first used in 1929) happens to be one of my all-time favorites. Over the course of that century, Coke has promised a horde of benefits such as purity, friendship, hospitality, convenience, and crisp taste. What about Pepsi? Similar pattern...72 years of Pepsi advertising have brought us 52 slogans.[4] How long do you think the folks at Nike will stick with "Just Do It?" It may surprise you, but 2014 marked that slogan's sixteenth birthday. "Just Do It" is still a teenager.

Advertising isn't what it used to be; television is fragmented and social media is interactive. Movies are at your fingertips, anywhere, any time. That's just the media side of advertising. The reach and frequency of a commercial have always been important to marketers, but media weight rarely determines the difference between success and failure of a campaign. The good news for small players is that the creative product itself is the prime driver of success or failure.

Absolut Vodka's long running "bottle" advertising is an exception to the revolving door of campaigns. It happens to be one of the most successful consumer products campaigns in the history of advertising—in the league of Volkswagen's "Think Small" and Nike's "Just Do It" persuasions. The original concept, created by Art Director Geoff Hayes in a bathtub and perpetuated by several creative notables, has helped establish the third largest-selling liquor brand on the globe. What is it that enables this remarkable campaign to live on when others died?

Rationally speaking, the campaign has unmistakably enhanced Absolut Vodka's imagery and profitability. I'm certain also that on the emotional side, the concept has motivated the next cohort of writers and art directors to unearth break-through avenues of execution within the boundaries of the advertising's best tenets. This campaign is a work of art, and the collection of ads is part of generational pop culture. That means free publicity.

Too often it is the marketers themselves that bring campaigns to hasty RIPs. Marketers operate in a dynamic world. When they change companies, they want to put their mark on the brands under their new roof. This leads to change for change's sake. I've seen it happen time and time again (never on my watch). Okay, you might say, what about the argument that "we should fix it before it breaks." Not in this case.

The longevity of the "bottle" campaign is not attributable to the long list of outstanding brand managers, copywriters, and art directors, notwithstanding their immeasurable contributions along the way. The ultimate credit lies within the executive management and culture of Sweden's V&S Group (owners until 1998) and Absolut's acquirer, Pernod Ricard. This is the secret to Absolut's success. This is what makes Absolut, absolute. The most senior folks in these two companies found the will and the way to push forward with strategic consistency and simplicity, keeping the campaign fresh and relevant to the target group. The economic prize for V&S's guidance and resolve turned out to be $8.9 billion from Pernod Ricard in the transaction.[5] Absolut could not have found a better replacement brand custodian.

"We will continue to raise our game so that creativity and innovation are the heart of our model," says the French liquor maker in their annual report. "In Absolut, creativity drives excellence—more inventive than ever, Absolut remains an inexhaustible source of inspiration and passion the world over for the most demanding artists and consumers." This is an emotionally powerful statement.

Advertising's creative talent pool may well be dwindling, but the very best artists and writers continue to be drawn to clients who worship at the Church of Brand.

Neck and Neck

Since the birth of rock 'n' roll in the fifties, the products of Fender Musical Instruments and the Gibson Guitar Corporation have dominated a global market enthralled with rock music and rock celebrities. From rec room pickers to Nashville professionals, Gibson and Fender are transcendental brands. Surprisingly, the folks who run these companies are not parishioners at the Church of Brand. Nonetheless, they continue to reap the rewards of brand annuities.

I'll explain the annuities this way: a consumer brand's longevity hinges on several success factors. For most companies, the marketing function is perched near the top. Think about marketing's role in creating and expanding L'Oreal, BMW, McDonald's, Ikea, American Express, and Disney. Every one of these companies traveled a road of opportunity paved by strategic vision and superb marketing execution. By contrast, Gibson and Fender's twenty-first-century performance on the scale of strategic vision and marketing aptitude has been woefully weak. How, then, do their brands remain successful icons of pop music globally?

My research into the workings of Fender and Gibson began with a website and social media search. Both websites are "sales oriented" and cluttered with dealer, product, and price list information. Their headline statements failed to tug at the heartstrings. I found no strategic messaging anywhere, nor any hints of either brand's positioning. Their Twitter and Facebook pages did not change my mind. Gibson's Twitter Page says, "Gibson is known worldwide for producing classic models in every major style of fretted instrument, including acoustic & electric guitars, mandolins & banjos." I've a hunch their 900,000+ Twitter followers already know this. Why not tell them what makes Gibson the best? Gibson's Facebook Page: "Musical Instrument." That's it.

Now to Fender's Twitter Page: "The official Twitter profile of Fender Musical Instruments—a.k.a. Fender Guitars." This wasted plot of real estate might explain why Fender's followers pale in comparison to Gibson's. Fender Facebook Page: "This is the official Fender® Facebook page! Where classics live, and dreams are born. Make history!" Eureka! "Where classics live, and dreams are born" is a terrific aspirational statement that plays off the brand's revered heritage, described by Fender as "Timeless Tradition." Maybe someone over at Fender is a marketer after all.

With a wealth of history to work with, you would think that the marketers at Gibson and Fender would have crafted slogans capable of touching the hearts and the heads of their current and future customers. The irony in all of this is a sensational 2006 YouTube video that beautifully depicts the painstaking art of Gibson guitar making.[6] Why this link isn't highlighted on the first page of Gibson's website baffles the mind.

In terms of product offerings, Gibson and Fender sing from the same songbook of unfocused and proliferated lineups. The last time I checked, Gibson's portfolio consisted of 341 electric guitars and 152 acoustics. Fender offered 520 guitar versions, of which 143 were Stratocasters, 106 were Telecasters, and 127 were various models of the electric bass.[7] Other than design and color, do you think it is possible to successfully differentiate 89 Fender Stratocasters? I'm betting that even Eric Clapton would have a difficult time distinguishing between the sound and finger action within the top ten and within the bottom ten. Forgive me if I ignore amplifier and accessory proliferation. I don't want to flog a dead horse.

Although the adeptness of a brand's marketing effort is generally determined by sales growth, market share, product/packaging innovation, and advertising, it is pricing strategy that is the clue to evaluation. Marketing low-price entries of premium brands isn't smart. Sure, cheapies with good brand names sell, and, yes, they expand the market. But what impact do they have on imagery and reputation, and what message does this strategic recklessness send to customers who have shelled out big bucks for the best? I suspect it is the same disappointing sentiment that top-of-the-line Mercedes Benz buyers feel when they see CLA-Class models selling for under $30,000.

In the discount category, Fender markets not one but three entries under the Fender Squire house brand—the Mini ($179), the Bullet ($199), and the Affinity ($279). And Fender's insatiable quest to sell more guitars at low prices does not stop there. The Stratocaster and Telecaster subbrands that retail for as much as $8,000 start at $559. Marketing blasphemy!

Gibson is the better of the bad duo at the discount game. They have chosen Epiphone as the brand that will offer both low- *and* high-price guitars. Epiphone guitars start at a couple of hundred dollars and go up to several thousand. You will need $499 before you can buy a guitar that is branded Gibson. And the price of Gibson's best? A cool $21,499 will make you the proud owner of their "most elegant, finely crafted arch top" called the Custom Citation.[8]

With all this branding ineptitude working against them, you must be wondering what in the world has made Gibson and Fender hugely successful? Is it unrivaled product quality? At the high end it could be, but there's a morgue of quality products dwelling in brand cemeteries because of poor marketing. Despite so many errant ways, the underlying factor for their success is this: rock star usage. You see, Fender and Gibson are the beneficiaries of massive indirect celebrity endorsements. Buddy Holly, Stevie Ray Vaughn, Jimi Hendrix, and Chet Atkins are all gone, but Mark Knopfler, Bruce Springsteen, Eric Clapton, Carlos Santana, and hundreds more live on.

The executives who run these organizations are the luckiest global brand marketers on the planet. I can't imagine how they'd survive in the tech industry.

Nonetheless, when two players dominate a market, there is always an opportunity for the entrepreneur. In the United States alone there are over 400 hand-crafted makers of acoustic and electric guitars. Every market offers an opportunity for the niche player. Here's a list of some of those niches: bluegrass, classical, harp style, flamenco, restoration, arch-top, custom, jazz, and heritage.

One high-end maker has been operating in America since the 1833. The family-owned and operated Martin Guitar Company, with 500+ employees, prides itself on crafting guitars with the quality ethic expressed by Frank Henry Martin in a 1904 catalogue. "How to build a guitar to give this tone is not a secret," Martin said. "It takes care and patience. Care in selecting the materials, laying out the proportions, and attending to the details which add to the player's comfort—patience in giving the necessary time to finish every part. A good guitar cannot be built for the price of a poor one, but who regrets the extra cost for a good guitar?"[9] This statement of policy, and the way Fender and Gibson operates, might explain Martin Guitar's longevity.

Old Brands, New Hands, Last Stands

The antithesis of Absolut Vodka and L'Oreal is a host of mismanaged or discarded stars of yesteryear. I realize I've been around a long time whenever I reminisce about the brands I was associated with in the early days of my career. A couple still thrive, but most are either shadows of their former selves or are six feet under. My first job was with Bristol-Myers, the maker of health and beauty aids Clairol, Bufferin, Excedrin, and Ban Deodorant. Back then, Bristol-Myers also produced several also-rans, such as Ipana and Fact Toothpaste, Vitalis Hair Tonic, Softique Bath Oil, and Mum and Trig Deodorant. Where are these also-rans now, and why?

Today, under Canadian dental products maker Maxill, Ipana Toothpaste's heart still pumps, but faintly. Maxill apparently has plans to resuscitate Ipana as a "retro brand" in the professional arena. Don't bet on success. As for Vitalis, trademark owner Helen of Troy looks to extend the brand's life with a range of line extensions that includes shampoos and conditioners. Line extensions, even on healthy brands, are not the panacea for sales and profit challenges. Mum Deodorant found its way to P&G as baggage with a number of other acquired Bristol-Myers beauty brands. It is now licensed to Doetsch Grether, which attempted but failed to benefit from Mum's 120-year heritage in a fancy European relaunch. And finally, there is Trig, Fact, and Softique, none of which bothered to reveal themselves on my Google obituary search.

Then there is this strategic twist. The company that now owns Brylcreem Hairdressing (at one time I was Brylcreem's brand manager at Beecham) is Combe Inc., founded by Ivan D. Combe in the 1940s. Family owned and operated, Combe sells several other falling stars such as Vagisil, Lectric Shave, Aqua Velva, Sea-Bond, and Johnson's Foot Soap. Until their website changed in 2012, Combe's slogan was "We're not a Me-Too Company; We're a What-If Company." They also claimed to be "innovative thinkers" who marketed "unique brands" to "loyal consumers." Keep in mind that their users have been around since the birth of network television. The former site made reference to the company's global growth. I wonder if the "growth" is due to this quality of strategic thinking from Combe: "People around the world have different cultures. They speak different languages. But our basic human problems are pretty much the same. Hair goes gray. Dentures slip. People itch. So everywhere on the globe where people have problems, Combe's brands grow. It's a great big world. And everywhere we look, we see new opportunities." Hmm. You might want to read that again. Now I ask you ... does this marketing wizardry have a chance at attracting sufficient numbers of consumers under the age of 60 to replace those with one foot in the grave?

Once a brand has fallen from the top three or four positions in its category, there isn't much hope for a successful restage. This is where you have to sacrifice a piece of your heart. You have to pull the life support plug to your darling(s). Yes, a dose of cosmetic surgery can delay the inevitable by temporarily extending the tarnished brand's life cycle. But, sure as God made little green apples, that brand is done. It is time to divest (as did Bristol Myers, Beecham, and P&G) or "milk" the brand rather than put more effort and more money into a lost cause. The funds and the time ought to go to the rising stars; keeping those stars bright is a better ROE and ROI. Having said that, I can't deny that my little darling's "little dab'll do ya" continues to occupy a warm place in my heart.

Don't Forget the Boomers

Before leaving memory lane, I want to address the burgeoning baby boomer market. I know a thing or two about this category because I am one of 80 million baby boomers born between 1946 and 1964 in Canada and the United States.

Our generation changed the modern world. We protested against war, discrimination, and censorship. Our values refused to accept injustice. Without us, America would never have elected a black-skinned president with a foreign name. England and Germany would never have elected female prime ministers. Canada would not have welcomed all creeds and colors into a land of multicultural liberty and opportunity. Encouraged by parents who suffered the hardships of a horrific world war, we worked hard to do better, to make something of ourselves. In their minds, "doing better" meant making a good living, holding a good job. Naturally, making money became our modus operandi. But along the way, we questioned the theory behind the almighty buck, contemplated values, grew independent, and blazed our own trail of social change.

Today, we represent a marvelous commercial opportunity. We dig in our heels and fight the advance of old age every inch of the way. We live by the "use it or lose it" mantra. And yes, we still have our insecurities.

"Aha," say the savvy marketers. The theme is familiar. As a young brand manager, I pounced on the public's insecurities, pumping products that solved bad breath, armpit odor, yellow teeth, and bad skin. That era represented the heyday of problem/solution brands such as the ones I referred to a couple of pages earlier. Now, we agonize over thinning hair, droopy skin, wrinkles around the eyes, and dysfunction below the belt. The world's best marketers are on to us. They also stick to the KISS theory of marketing. Harley-Davidson promises us two-wheel freedom of the sixties on their iconic Fat Boy. They know we can well afford it. So do Pfizer and Eli Lilly, the makers of Viagra and Cialis.

To all marketers, I say this on behalf of baby boomers: go ahead, help us fulfill our lifestyle aspirations. Give us the means, and you will reap the reward of a loyal customer happy to pay premium prices for your well-differentiated products and services. But, please...never mention "old age" in your persuasion.

Social Media and the Little Guy

Not since television's debut has anything impacted marketing more than the social media tsunami. Who would have thought that product and service promises broadcast to the masses would be trumped by conversations between the manufacturer, their brand, and the individual consumer? Social media is about connecting people; it is not about planting a problem in the viewer's mind and jamming the solution down his or her throat via a 30-second television commercial. As for the adaptation of this new medium by old-school marketers . . . many are resisting. Not P&G, a branding pioneer. If in doubt, all you have to do is Google the Old Spice Social Media Case Study.[10]

My fascination with social media is rooted in the opportunity it presents to small business. Devoid of massive budgets, unknown brands and businesses can play in the big leagues by competing with an arsenal of nimbleness and creativity. The right idea, sincerity of purpose, and superior KISS execution that isn't in your face can firmly endear any brand or company to the chosen market.

The "not in your face" type of thinking and engagement with customers is precisely Chobani Yogurt's approach to social media. Chobani is active on Facebook, Twitter, and Pinterest, the most visual of the mediums with a fertile demographic and psychographic audience. Chobani's boards include inspirational quotes on a "Nothing but Good" board, and motivational quotes on a "Chobani Fit" board. While the content has no direct relation to the product itself, it helps define Chobani as a force for good, and a force for health and fitness.

Small businesses capitalizing on the social media opportunity run the gamut from artisans to undertakers. For them, social media offers low-cost broad or narrow reach, depending on the targeted traffic. Social media is getting bigger and stronger—

the sooner small players are in, the sooner they will enjoy the returns. If you're a small player, do it now.

Chapter 6 Summary

- Differentiation is still the name of the marketing game. Distinction in service, image, and promise allows a brand to occupy a piece of the busy mind.
- You don't stumble upon marketing insight. You have burrow for it and then conceptualize it.
- If you want differentiation, you have to ask yourself this question: what am I prepared to sacrifice to get it?
- Creating a new brand from scratch and watching it grow is the most fulfilling experience a marketer will ever realize. There is plenty of room in this world to do that. But stick to the tenets of KISS.
- Advertisers get the kind of advertising they deserve.
- When a brand has fallen from the number three or four position within its category, there isn't much hope for a restage. Milk it, polish it up, and kiss it goodbye.
- Baby boomers are a fertile target group for today's savvy marketers.
- In social media, it is the idea, the purpose, and the execution that endear a brand or a company to the customer.

CHAPTER 7

Bastions of Branding

Never in the history of marketing has there been so much talk about branding. The conversation is well beyond product and service brand discussion by marketers and ad agencies. Branding has flourished big time—we now have personal brands, country brands, political brands, cause-related brands, even cultural brands. The ramification is clutter, the adversary of brand identity. So wouldn't you expect a heck of a lot more corporate attention to commercial brands? Wouldn't you expect greater care in stamping out complexity and stewarding brand presence, personality, positioning, single-mindedness, and strategic consistency?

Richard Branson, Jeff Bezos, John MacKay, Tony Hsieh, and Phil Knight offer a guiding light. They are members of a small club of founders, CEOs, and board chairs whose names are synonymous with well-known trademarks that do not bear their names. I consider them great brand custodians because they are fanatical about the process of branding—their convictions a contrast to those with a fervent focus on the value of the brand asset. By any standard, their businesses aren't small, but these leaders are awfully good at keeping complexity at bay and doing less, better. Within their particular markets (and in some cases on a much more pervasive basis), these men are the brand.

The phenomenon of "leader as the brand" has moved beyond the spokesman roles of Colonel Harland Saunders (KFC), Juan Valdez (Columbia Coffee Growers), and Bill Cosby (Jell-O). Sure, some of the members of this small club of founders, CEOs, and/or board chairs who exert a powerful influence on their company's trademarks are colorful celebrities, but more importantly, they continue to be active advocates of nurturing and protecting the DNA of their companies' most valued assets. Within their own DNA is a passion to ensure that brand strategy and execution are congruent with the strategic intentions and cultural values of their vision.

Fun-loving Richard Branson has built the Virgin brand around his reputation. The proof is in Virgin's uncanny ability to enter so many categories and carve out success. Branson manages to negate the complexity of a conglomerate by keeping his companies as simple as possible, operating them as autonomous, manageable enterprises. As for failures in cola, clothing, movies, and vodka, I doubt he loses a wink of sleep over them. You have to break a few eggs to make an omelet.

The now-chair of Nike's board, Phil Knight is best known for linking the spirit of American pop culture to sports by capitalizing on the public's idolization of athletic heroes. He did this by putting faith in an endorsement strategy that created the quintessential aspirational brand. Ever since "Just do it," Nike shoes have bolstered their functional product benefits with emotional payoffs. That's the secret to their brand power. Knight is another leader who isn't shy about pruning. Not long ago, Umbro and Cole Hann were set loose to facilitate greater focus on the Nike brand of athletic apparel and footwear.

Howard Schultz is known for revolutionizing coffee around the world. In 2008, he returned from the sidelines to take the company and the brand to a new level. That meant geographical expansion and product line expansion. It's the latter expansion that challenges the reputation of the brand, and Howard knows it. "Our history is based on extending the brand to categories within the guardrails of Starbucks, but the key to success is to remain true to the brand, and not abuse the trust people have by going off and doing things not consistent with the heritage of coffee."[1] I liked hearing that from Howard in 2013, but I'm not so sure the movie business or chocolate beverage failures will limit Starbuck's zest for product line proliferation. I'm still choking on the instant coffee made by Starbucks.

Jeff Bezos treats the Amazon brand as though it were a person. As such, he is a strong proponent and guardian of Amazon's reputation. A reputation is earned by trying to do hard things well. This ethic pervades Amazon's operations. Until recently, Bezos was often heard saying, "Sacrifice the present for a better future." He can thank patient investors for believing in his prophecy.

Red Bull's Dietrich Mateschitz is a superb example of "leader as the brand." Mateschitz has an intimate knowledge of what Red Bull is and what it is not. In his mind, nurturing the Red Bull image is the key to remaining leader in the energy drink business. As you know, Mateschitz has done that very, very well.

Guy Laliberté of Cirque du Soleil started out busking as an accordion player, stilt walker, and fire eater before founding this amazing entertainment company and creating a language with universal appeal. He is testament to the fact that you don't need an MBA to succeed in business. Lately, Laliberté has been doing more pruning than planting—cutting back shows, streamlining operations, and doing less, better by focusing on fewer, bigger productions, such as "Michael Jackson: The Immortal World Tour," which boasts annual ticket sales of over $100 million.

John Mackey is synonymous with natural foods and conscious capitalism—the philosophy of operating a business with a social purpose. He has no qualms about making money, but says that purpose is not particularly inspiring. The contribution he makes to others is what turns his crank. John Mackey is the Whole Foods brand.

Tony Hsieh believes that the culture and the brand are inseparable. This might explain his strong conviction for hiring the right mind-sets. Although Zappos has been acquired by Amazon, Hsieh remains Zappos' chief executive. Expect him to continue championing the belief that customer service should never be a department; rather, it should be the company.

It's hard to find a CEO of P&G who doesn't believe in great marketing and branding. A.G. Lafley headed P&G from 2000 to 2009, and then came out of retirement in 2013 to reignite the juggernaut. I challenge you to find a consumer packaged goods CEO who is so passionate about design. "Design," he says, "is as important as the materials that go into a new product, and is critical to innovation and building brand equity. It is part of the communication of a brand name and brand promise. Design is an area where we have to have core capability. We want to elevate it, invest in it and make it a core competence."[2] I think A.G. took a page out of Steve Jobs' book. The branding beliefs and disciplines of this CEO help explain the increasing visibility of P&G's products and the reputation of P&G as a great company—more on that in the next chapter.

There are scads of CEOs who talk branding, but few inject themselves into the brand and leave a legacy anywhere close to Branson, Knight, Schultz, Bezos, Mateschitz, Laliberté, Mackey, Hsieh, and Lafley. If you think they succeeded as great brand custodians without exercising strategic sacrifice, think again.

At the other end of the equation are chief executives who continually talk about brand assets, but do little to enhance them—they take the easy road, choosing to live off the luster of yesteryear's brand equity—extending their trademarks into unrelated categories. Sure, they endorse a whack of dough into media, but they are not spearheading brand equity growth. They are diminishing it.

Kellogg's has fallen into the trap of bigger is better. I have been a big fan of this company since I was an account executive at Leo Burnett Advertising Agency. The brand and company name stood for healthy breakfasts, and for decades their adept, disciplined marketers worked hard at fortifying that stellar reputation. This fine work established Special K as a healthy, nutritious breakfast for diet-conscious women.

Like Campbell's, Kellogg's, with a stagnating top- and bottom line and investor pressures, decided to spread their corporate

wings. It is one thing to diversify, as they did with their acquisitions of Keebler and Pringles, but quite another to exploit a
valuable brand asset by slapping "K" on products that fail to
build or live up to Special K's core positioning. This is the opposite of sacrifice—this is sacrilege.

I see the wisdom of nutritious granola and cereal bars, but the
recent launches of cracker chips and flatbread breakfast sandwiches under the name Special K goes too far. Special K Cracker
Chips contain 110 calories per 30-gram serving. This is mar-
ginally less than Frito Lay's 127 calories for the same weight.
Flatbread sandwiches may be 40 percent fewer calories than
McDonald's version, but they are still a combo of cholesterol,
fat, and sodium that won't do you any good.

Q: What is Kellogg's marketing justification? A: The product
is better for the diet than those of the competition. The truth is
in the economics. Kellogg's will sell more flatbread sandwiches
under the name Special K than it would under Eggo or another
brand name from their stable.

Further justification can be found in Kellogg's 2011 annual
report. "The Kellogg Company has always sought to provide
foods that are enjoyable and nutritious. However, we also recognize that consumers seek different things from different brands."[3]
Aha. This helps explain the company's new vision—enrich and
delight the world through foods and brands that matter. Does
"brands that matter" imply that Kellogg's will make whatever
the customer wants? For all intents and purposes, there is nothing wrong with the philosophy, provided a superb brand asset is
not maligned as the means to that end.

The new economy has learned the lessons of branding discipline rather well. Beyond Bezos and Hsieh, there are plenty
of CMOs and CEOs who recognize the necessity of their own
direct and passionate involvement as chief brand custodians.
This top management ethic is essential to brand resilience. With
the exception of niche, specialty, and some consumer technology

markets, I see less and less of this in big business. There's a smorgasbord of reasons why great brands and great companies lose their way. The trouble often starts with brand management itself—the loss of direction, the inability to inject innovation, the failure to recognize customer evolution, the lack of understanding of what the brand is and what it is not. These are the symptoms that have punished fallen stars such as Hostess, Barnes & Noble, Kodak, and Radio Shack.

Not so long ago, Sony looked invincible. In 2013, they made a small profit after four consecutive years of losses. Sony is comprised of three main businesses: electronics, entertainment, and financial services. Recently, they shelled out $1.8 billion for a mishmash of businesses ranging from medical equipment to cloud gaming. Kaz Hirai, Sony's CEO, has a strategy to rebuild the problematic electronics business. He thinks there is clarity in concentrating on gaming, digital imaging, and mobile devices. To me, gaming, digital imaging, and mobile devices seem awfully broad. Sacrifice or doing less, better doesn't appear in the tea leaves. Nor does strategy, the most misused and misunderstood word in business.

Sony's modest profit in 2013 was the result of margin gains from devaluation in the yen and improved performance from the financial services and the movie divisions.[4] With the core electronics business continuing to struggle, strategic health remains tenuous.

Hirai thinks the Sony DNA is "a distinctive will and drive to generate new value."[5] I searched the information network, but came up empty-handed with regard to this CEO's views on what the brand stands for in the customer's mind. However, he did say that if Sony can't deliver a great consumer experience on the product front, the brand will take a ding. That's an understatement.

Chief executives who wake up to the reality of neglected brand assets, and who are prepared to take corrective action to surgically reinvigorate them must ensure they have the best, most experienced marketing and creative talent in the operating room. They must also commit to being fused at the hip with these renewal experts and prepared to champion the surgery as well as the convalescence.

Spending more money in media and promotion without corrective strategic action isn't the prescription for the ailment. If this were effective, Campbell's soups would not have languished in stagnation for so many years. Once a brand has undergone radical surgery, rather than a cosmetic facelift, that brand will be armed with a viable rationale for seeking the funds to communicate relevant and tangible promises. It is only at this stage that today's customers will be ready to listen.

Brand Positioning Durability

We are members of a community that loves lists—the registries you read or hear about in the first or second month of every year. Consumer rags boost circulation by pumping out "lists" of the sexiest, the best and worst dressed, the best places to live, the most popular cars, even the lottery's unluckiest or unhappiest winners. Business periodicals rank the top 500 companies according to turnover, profit, brand value, innovation, and work climate. CEO lists are increasingly popular. You can find lists of the best or worst performing, the highest paid, the most powerful women CEOs, and, thanks to the Bernie Madoffs of the corporate world, a top 10 list of crooked CEOs.

If I were to ask you to list the five most distinctive brand icons of all time, what symbols would make your list? I suspect this question conjures up several iconic images and personas. Some of you will visualize a white calligraphic script on a shiny-red circular background, a single checkmark, or two yellow vertical arcs. Brands, to most people, are consumable goods and services made by companies. With all their marketing muscle, our brains are wedged in a commercial paradigm of brands such a Coca-Cola, Nike, and McDonald's.

Many of these famous names were conceived within our lifetimes, and as long as marketers persist in adding value to these assets, their trademarks will be around for generations to come. Now, I'd like you to identify the longest-lasting, most durable international brand icons that were not created by companies, industries or not-for-profit organizations. When I went through this exercise myself, I settled on five marks that passed the most stringent torture test of any brand—an enduring, well-differentiated brand platform. Each of these icons represents unique and indelible positions in the minds of hundreds of million human beings. But don't expect any of them to be on 2014's list of the world's best brands, particularly brand icon number five.

1. *The Christian Cross*. This symbol has stood for the Christian faith since the second century. Two thousand years later, the positioning is unchanged, and to many, its emotional power is as strong as ever.
2. *The Star of David* was first used in the eleventh century. There isn't an icon that embodies the Jewish identity like it.
3. *The Statue of Liberty* is distinctively American. This monument in the middle of New York's harbor is the nation's symbol of democratic freedom for people of all creeds and colors.
4. *The Olympic Rings* have stood for global athletic unification since 1914.
5. *The Swastika*. The sight of the swastika brings discomfort to most of us, but we cannot deny its positioning clarity. For generations to come, Hitler's rebranding of the 3,000-year-old symbol will be associated with discrimination, suffering, and death.

Human emotion is inherent in all of these world marks. Personal brands and business brands seek to capture their target group's heartstrings, but compared to these historical icons, nothing compares.

Great Slogans Do Less, Better

So what is it about the three or four words that embed a brand's single-minded promise into the minds of the customer? We've all heard clever catchphrases. How many of them are consistent with the brand's features and pertinent to the intended target. Slogan sustainability is contingent on relevance. You already know from the previous chapter that the two largest cola brands on the face of the earth have collectively gone through more than a 100 slogans in a hundred years. The product hasn't changed much has it? So, beyond sound strategic reasoning for change, an existing slogan's life span is at the mercy of the marketer's boredom, sluggish sales, or a copywriter's great idea for the next tagline.

When companies decide that it is time for a new slogan, the marketing team evaluates several new catchphrase candidates by a defined set of objectives. People who do not understand marketing and branding will assess the line purely by its cleverness or impact. This is a colossal mistake that happens all the time. Slogans must be judged the same way as advertising is judged. Make sure you have the concise written brand strategy in front of you. This is a brief document that has been discussed and approved by senior management and endorsed by the creative agency. As in the "Step into Action" charity example, the strategy states what you want the slogan to say about your brand.

Begin the assessment by ensuring that the candidates communicate that strategy. If a contender fails to pass this test of strategic intent, stop. Do not bother judging that particular slogan against the other criteria. The fact that it works well with an advertising execution is irrelevant. The tag line must pass the strategy test. When it does, you are ready to appraise the cleverness of the creative, the fit with the brand's personality, the emotional and rational appeal, and the all-important staying power.

The most successful slogan that I was associated with was for Nabob Coffee in Canada. When rival Maxwell House matched our vacuum packaging technology, we were left without a tangible point of difference other than our particular blend of beans. The marketing team and the J. Walter Thompson advertising agency decided that we needed a lasting positioning for Nabob—one that could stand for the flagship brand and yet not infringe upon any new technology breakthroughs such as single-serve pods or reusable coffee filters. We settled on positioning Nabob as the coffee that took the most care to select only the best beans for its blends. The inherent payoff, of course, was the delicious, steaming nectar in the cup.

Initially, I thought "Many are Picked, Few are Chosen" was too long and cumbersome. There was also some discussion that people might object to its similarity to "many are called but few are chosen" from the book of Matthew. That concern didn't last long. The line was so strategically powerful that we went with it, and for many years, the "best beans" strategy solidified Nabob's leadership position. The slogan died when Kraft purchased Jacobs Suchard. However, to Kraft's credit (and as you know by now, I seldom give Kraft credit), they stayed with the bean strategy, modifying it to "Better Beans, Better Coffee." Perhaps Kraft's brand managers were worried that the consumer wasn't bright enough to make the connection. "Better Beans, Better Coffee" is certainly less verbose and easier to remember. But that slogan won't be remembered, because it was changed in 2014 to "Respect the Bean."

Kraft, in their zeal to put their own stamp on the brand, overlooked the emotional steel of "Many are Picked, Few are Chosen." Like the advertising campaign that ran for ten years, this slogan exemplified the demanding and uncompromising brand personality that we built into Nabob Coffee. Demanding and uncompromising also happened to be the corporate culture of our company. Fancy that.

As for the perfect slogan, I consider these five are as good as it gets:

1. *Just Do It*. Frankly, I'm not so sure I would have approved this line back in 1988. I know my juices would have been stirred by the call to action, the simplicity and the possibility of staying power. But without the benefit of an advertising campaign to visualize and communicate the slogan's strategic purpose, "Just Do It" would have been a tough sell. That's history. "Just Do It" proved to be an awesome way to bond the consumer to the Nike lifestyle.

2. *Breakfast of Champions*. Created in 1935, this slogan wins the endurance race, hands down. And like "Just Do It," the phrase connects the consumer to the athlete, and the athlete to the product. To reinforce the brand promise, General Mills began featuring athletes on the Wheaties box in 1958. They're still doing it.

3. *A Diamond is Forever* was launched in 1948. Today, the only knock against this tagline is the association to De Beers. Over time, the slogan has become generic to the market. Is this the fault of the slogan or the fault of the marketer? From a commercial perspective, the point is moot. As go diamonds, so goes De Beers. Hmm. That's not such a bad slogan, either.

4. *You're in Good Hands*. Insurance companies sell "peace of mind," and Allstate captured this beautifully with the line and a potent visual of a house cradled in the caring palms of two hands. Ironically, the slogan was not created by an ad agency but by an Allstate sales manager in 1950. Living up to the promise is another matter, and Allstate has plenty of work to do in this regard.

5. *Finger Lickin' Good.* Although this line was replaced by KFC after more than a half century of use, it remains one of my favorites. From a food-centric standpoint, the slogan is rational, but more importantly, the imagery of licking fingers delivers the emotional hook. It can make one's mouth water. According to KFC, the new slogan "So Good," is more holistic, applying to staff and service, as well as food.[6] Adding the objectives of staff and culture into a slogan that is meant to inspire customers is another example of a company's trying to do more and more with a slogan, than doing less, better. "So Good" is in the league of "Tastes Best," scoring zero on the emotional, mouth-watering barometer.

As for honorable mentions, kudos to BMW for "The Ultimate Driving Machine," AMEX for "Don't Leave Home without It," and Coca-Cola for "The Pause that Refreshes." I'd like to think that "Mastery under Glass" will be a contender one day. That slogan happens to be the one I created for Casey Houweling's greenhouse operation.

The Brand Name Hall of Fame

To round out the "best lists" in this chapter, I am going to leave you with my all-time favorite brand names, judged according to a novel criterion. In the assessment, I have purposely ignored brand reputation, as well as a brand's pecking order within the market, and the graphic treatment of its logo and package. When you clear the slate and imagine a brand at inception, before advertising, before promotion, and before beautiful packaging graphics, you have before you the cleanest and purest criterion for choosing an outstanding nomenclature. You have to imagine what it could be.

For the most part, the thread connecting my selection is product association, imagery, character (personality), and differentiation as conveyed by the name. Some of these factors would rule out Zappos, Starbucks, Nintendo, Amazon, and eBay, notwithstanding what these notables have done with the products that carry their names. My measurement criterion may seem like a lot to ask in one word or two. With few exceptions, the brand names on my list deliver on every one of these attributes before a dollar needed to be spent on advertising, design, and promotion. Yet, because some of the brand owners failed to prudently invest in their asset, a few of these favorites have fallen to the cruel test of time.

10. *Wrangler.* With product features that were designed to appeal to cowboys, Wrangler jeans have stood for genuine western wear since they were introduced in the 1940s. Sadly, Wrangler faced mounting competition, closed its last American sewing plant in 2005, and slipped from the apex into a gorge of lost consumer esteem.

9. *Southern Comfort.* Created in 1874 by a New Orleans bartender, the Southern Comfort name delivers cult-like emotional imagery and promises a taste pleasure unique to the American South.

8. *Häagen-Dazs.* This name violates my "product association" rule. It also proves that I am not stubborn to the ridiculous. Häagen-Dazs is two made-up words meant to look Scandinavian to the American eye. The name is so strong on imagery, character, and mystique that I was willing to overlook its missing product association.

7. *Mike's Hard Lemonade.* The brand and vodka lemonade category was invented by Don Chisholm of Vancouver's Dossier Creative. Chisholm brilliantly positioned Mike's as an emotionally engaging, antimarketing, irreverent brand. One of the most creative brand names ever, Mike's is the best example of a brand that became a phenomenal success years before a penny was spent on advertising.

6. *Champion*. The name smacks of power and accomplishment. At one time, the spark plug maker was a Fortune 500 Company. While Champion's awareness remains high among auto and racing enthusiasts, the brand has stumbled and fallen to the canvas. It is unlikely to get up.

5. *Wonder*. Rumor has it that baking executive Elmer Cline was filled with wonder by the scene of hundreds of red, yellow, and blue balloons at the 1921 Indianapolis International Balloon Race. I've always loved this brand name, although I'm the first to admit that Wonder Bread failed to deliver the wonderment of taste, texture, or nutrition.

4. *Dove*. Superficially, Dove is the simplest and most unimaginative brand name on my list. Emotionally, it is hard to beat. A dove symbolizes peacefulness, gentleness, purity, and softness—that's what women want for their hair and their skin.

3. *Walkman*. The original Sony Walkman audio player transformed music listening habits by delivering the convenience of portable music. Walkman did not describe the product; rather, it told you what you could do with it. The name trumps iPod. The trick, of course is to remember that there is far more to a brand's success than the name.

2. *DieHard*. DieHard is an outstanding brand name whose best years are behind it. The battery's promise was a lifetime guarantee—that is, for as long as the customer owned the car in which it was originally installed. Inherent in the name is rugged masculinity, a "never give up" personality, and outstanding memorability.

1. *The Beetle*. The most fascinating aspect of the bug is that its name emanated from the public and not the company. Through word of mouth, The Käfer ("Beetle" in German) became the Volkswagen Beetle worldwide. The absurdity of this iconic name is that it never appeared in advertising or in Volkswagen printed material until 1968—a half century after introduction.

Are These Suds for You?

Beer markets offer so many lessons in branding. Locally and globally, maintaining the resiliency of a beer brand is as exciting as it is challenging. But once your brand is on the outs with the prime target group, cardiac arrest isn't far off. Oh sure, everyone tries to resuscitate their beloved brand with scads of Hail Mary endeavors ranging from cool package design to edgy advertising and fun-loving national promotions.

Marketers of Michelob, Fosters, Miller Genuine Draft, Black Label, and Labatt's 50 have all played at this game. All have battled tough odds to maintain mass brand appeal over the long haul. Labatt 50 Ale used to be the leading brand in Canada. A generation later, young beer drinkers started calling it "Dad's beer." Two generations later, Labatt 50 became "Granddad's beer." Labatt asked if I could help. "Afraid not," I said. The gig was up for good.

Experienced marketers ought to know by now that it is far better to milk the cow than flog the dead horse. The key to success in beer marketing is keeping the brand fresh. This is easier said than done. Marketers continue to seek that creative silver bullet, and once in a while an ad agency nails it, with outstanding creativity that imbeds the brand with the right emotional imagery at the right target group. Last year, Carlsberg's Belgian agency, Duval Guillaume Modem, introduced the concept of putting regular people through stressful predicaments and then disclosing the sting. They began with a cinema full of rugged, leather-clad bikers and followed that up with calls to a friend in the middle of the night asking for money to get them out of a poker game with a host of unsavory characters.

Great creative such as this is the vehicle to extend Carlsberg's life cycle in every market in which it competes. The challenge facing Carlsberg and every other long-standing beer brand, including Budweiser, is how to hit a home run every time. Even Babe Ruth couldn't do that.

Valued at $19 billion by Forbes and ranked number 23 on the World's Most Powerful Brand list, Anheuser-Busch InBev's non-US volume continues to make modest gains. But on its home turf, Bud faces tough times. The mother ship is now the number three brand behind Bud Light and Coors Light in a domestic market that has suffered 23 consecutive years of consumption decline.

Bud's marketers keep working hard at doing more of the same and trying to do it better. The approach isn't working. A-B is in a similar position to another great Americana brand that suffered stagnation as recently as 2010. Harley-Davidson rose from the ashes decades ago, and they are well on their way to doing it again.

Social Media and Brand Positioning Laziness

Any marketer can play the social media game and do it well with the right concept—you don't have to have the bank account of Unilever or Nestlé. What bothers me is the conspicuous deficiency in online advice on brand positioning within this exciting medium. People talk the numbers far more than they talk the content's branding objectives. They also assume that when a person talks about brand positioning, he or she wants to sell rather than engage. This is not necessarily the case.

Recently, I Googled the term "social media & strategy." The top links were checklists of "need-to-knows" about how to implement a social media strategy—generic stuff such as everyone working together, ascertaining senior management endorsement, engaging users, maintaining presence, and measuring performance. Searching "branding & social media" wasn't much better. The top link was a blog on the Twitter brand, and the next link spelled out the digital options such as Facebook, Twitter, and LinkedIn. Finally, I typed in "social media and brand positioning." That turned up an insightful five-year-old blog by Francois Gossieaux of Corante, a blog media company. "Pundits," purported Gossieaux, "will tell you to do away with brand messaging and positioning altogether, since it can't be controlled anyway. Not so fast! People need to know what bucket to put your offering in, and if they can't, they won't know how to assign value to what you have to offer."[7]

This guy nailed it. Ignoring brand positioning in social media is not only misguided, but is also laziness disguised by the premise that single-mindedness stifles social media opportunity. I say, stick to your brand positioning, but search for various interesting touchpoints to support and further entrench that positioning with your customers. As an example, a coffee brand with a "best beans" positioning could be guided along an assortment of avenues in the hypersocial world. The social media marketer could pursue the demanding personality of the brand to search out and secure superior coffee beans, travelogues of coffee-producing countries, idiosyncrasies of the tasters/blenders/customers, tidbits on varietals, analogies to wines, roasting, grinding, recipes, even the types of people who buy the brand.

Chobani is onto this in Pinterest. P&G remains committed to brand positioning and differentiation in all social media. Like so many other disciplines, this is institutionalized throughout P&G's marketing teams. Other companies, especially those with little brand management training or experience, are not as mindful about clear and simple brand strategies. The marketers in these organizations have allowed the consumer to define their strategy. That's a bad idea. The result will be mush.

Chapter 7 Summary

- Brands need fanatical brand custodians at the helm. These are the leaders who enjoy the long-term benefits of watching their brands and companies thrive.

- Brands can offer functional benefits, but the distinct identity that stimulates a meaningful emotional response is the strategic core of all branding—personal, business, nation, political, and cause related.
- A slogan that single-mindedly brings a brand's positioning to life ought to live a long live.
- As a general rule, the strategic goals that should be considered when choosing a brand name are product association, imagery, character (personality), and differentiation.
- Prudent brand positioning in social media need not stifle customer engagement. Those who operate by this fable are misguided, ignorant, or lazy. Maybe all three.

CHAPTER 8

Fewer, Better People Doing Less, Better

Without leadership, a business enterprise will eventually perish. Survival is possible without a strategy, but seldom over the long haul. Great strategy with lousy execution isn't worth the piece of paper it is written on. The consequence of these assertions is obvious. Get it right, bring it all together, and you have economic magic. The glue that binds these elements is people—quality individuals at the board level, in the C-suite, in the office, on the factory floor, and out there in the field.

Until the information age, companies needed hordes of people to run machines in plants and warehouses all over the country. The assets their shareholders valued most were tangible. Today, 80 percent of the assets of the Standard & Poor's 500 are intangible. These assets cannot be seen, touched, or physically measured. The knowledge economy appreciates the fact that trade secrets, trademarks, patents, knowledge, and know-how are what counts. This is why they spend so much on research and development. In 2013, the world's top 20 R&D spenders dished out $159 billion, a 4.4 percent increase compared to year ago.[1] Seven of these companies participated in the health-care sector, five in computers or electronics, five in automobile manufacturing, and two in software and the Internet.

Competitive intangibles are the source from which competitive advantage flows or goes, and human capital is the means and the end of these intangibles. Finding the best people, motivating them, retaining them, and facilitating their personal and professional development is never easy. CEOs come and go. Wall Street demands quarterly results. Recessions thrash thoughtful strategic intent and pressure CEOs into a hodgepodge of tactical "quick-fix" solutions. If these leaders are not careful, chaos will arise in the complexity they create.

Fewer, better people are a priceless asset. This doesn't have to mean a sweat shop environment. A lean team wards off the complexity cancer because the team maintains a focus on those activities that make a difference. They milk or kill past darlings and feed new blood into the veins of brands and businesses that will deliver superior results. Every leader should be zealous about finding the best talent. If you are in a position to determine remuneration, I suggest you pay them more than your competitors; the cost to the company will be less. High productivity creates high sales and profit-per-employee ratios.

Bureaucracies, in particular government agencies, have a habit of dealing with more projects by throwing more people at those projects. Earlier, I shared my experience with the government-controlled British Columbia Lottery Corporation. In British Columbia, the lottery is a monopoly—all legal gaming comes under its jurisdiction. When I joined the board of directors in 2001, the organization operated within a "more and more" culture, without too much worry about the expense of getting the job done. I understood why: no competition, and margins so lucrative that incremental staffing was seen as a drop in the bucket.

This point of view created too many projects, too many marginal brands, and a bloated organization to support several questionable activities. Complexity and fragmentation were holding this company back from realizing its true potential.

Well, squeaky wheels get the grease. I hounded management about head count and focus, and with the support of the board and a CEO who was prepared to go this way, the corporation pinpointed the various businesses and brands in which to prune

Table 8.1 British Columbia Lottery Revenue, Profit and Headcount

	Fiscal 05/06	Fiscal 12/13	Change
Revenue	$2.26 billion	$2.73 billion	+21%
Net Income	$0.92 billion	$1.13 billion	+23%
Employees	575	925	+60%

and in which to invest time and money. Over the course of my tenure, a refocused and reenergized management team accelerated revenue and profit without increasing staffing. People were doing less, much better.

Seven years have passed since I moved on, and that culture has dispersed like a whiff of smoke in a gentle breeze. A couple of changes in the corner office and new board members with different viewpoints have allowed employment growth to exponentially outpace revenue and profit growth. Numbers don't lie (see Table 8.1).

If your company's revenues were growing by less than 3 percent per year, would you be increasing staff levels by 7 percent each and every year? For the record, there are excellent people working at this organization, and many from my day are still there. But talent without leadership is like spitting into the wind. More vice-presidents, directors, and managers *doing more and more* do not make for a better business. Fewer vice-presidents, directors, and managers, operating under the *do less, better* strategy, make for a better business.

When to Sacrifice Your Pride

One of my favorite "inspirational" books is *The Art of Possibility* by Rosamund and Benjamin Zander. Although I read this book years ago, one situation stands out in my mind. Ben, at that time the conductor of the Boston Philharmonic, was teaching a master class at a festival in England. One of his students (Jeffrey) was working on a Schubert opera that told the story of a jilted lovesick man who knew that his love was lost forever.

"The music," wrote Ben, "is some of the most intimate, soft, subtle, and delicate in the repertoire. But when Jeffrey began to sing, there was no trace of melancholy. Out poured a glorious stream of rich, resonant, Italianate sound. Pure Jeffrey, taking himself very seriously. How could I induce him to look past himself in order to become a conduit for the expressive passion of the music? I began by asking if he was willing to be coached."

The young tenor said he was open to this.

"I engaged in a battle royal," said Ben, "not with Jeffrey but with his pride, his training, his need to look good, and the years of applause he had received for his extraordinary voice. As each layer was peeled away and as he got closer to the raw vulnerability of Schubert's distraught lover, his voice lost its patina and began to reveal the human soul beneath. His body, too, began to take on a softened and rounded turn. At the final words, "When will I have my lover in my arms again?" Jeffrey's voice, now almost inaudible, seemed to reach us through some other channel than sound. Nobody stirred—the audience, the players, the BBC crew—all of us were unified in silence. Then, finally, tremendous applause. Whenever someone gives up their pride to reveal a truth to others, we find it incredibly moving."[2]

I didn't realize that this passage would be such an enduring story about sacrifice. In Jeffery, Zander had an extremely talented individual who finally came to terms with his ego. He sacrificed it for a higher cause—the enjoyment of his audience. This is a great lesson for business leaders. Leave your egos in the parking lot. Come into the office, the factory, or the store ready to unleash the power of strategic sacrifice. You won't be sorry.

Honor the Unsung Heroes

In the pharmaceutical industry, the scientists who develop patentable breakthrough drugs are the heroes. A patent is the pot of gold to the big drugmakers, which invest millions of research dollars in new drug development. No wonder their CEOs and corporate boards tend to discount the value of the thousands of average Joes who work in their offices, factories, and warehouses.

Average Joes constitute the majority of workforces. Because they aren't categorized as whiz kids or water walkers, it's easy to take them for granted. This is a colossal mistake. Applaud them. Listen to them. Nurture their talent. Take pleasure in watching the difference these unsung heroes bring to a company. Clarity from strategic sacrifice can enhance every employee's purpose. The more specialized a company, the greater the discipline of the workforce. The unsung heroes know what the organization is trying to do, and they understand the role they can play in helping the company achieve its objectives.

I don't care whether or not the majority of the workforce is unionized. If nonunion employees are on a bonus plan, their trade union partners should be too. This may be easier said and done, because union negotiators don't trust bonus plans. You have to settle on the terms of the contract and then add the bonus element. They can't say "no" to this. Do it, and you are on your way to better performance, especially when you give a monetary "thank you" to every employee at the end of a successful fiscal year.

I had the pleasure of working with hundreds of unsung heroes. Here are the stories of just five of them.

Ronnie, a union employee, never missed the company Christmas party or the summer social event. Ronnie was an organizer—a leader in cultural development. Ronnie refused to be blocked by the rock wall that separates managements and unions. This guy took a sledgehammer to that wall and turned it to rubble. And through that wall came a hundred others. Why? Because company management believed in Ronnie, cared about Ronnie, and helped Ronnie understand why camaraderie in the workforce is a powerful competitive advantage for the company.

Bruce, an energetic marketing manager who struggled with detail on occasion, flourished as a brilliant creative resource. Bruce masterminded the sponsorship of a major nationwide charitable endeavor. When paraplegic athlete Rick Hansen returned to Canada after wheeling around the world to promote spinal cord research and raise funds, Bruce's promotion increased our coffee sales by 3 share points. This guy knew the impact that creativity had on a business with fewer resources than its competitors. This was how Bruce would make his difference.

Gary, an ex-marine middle manager, known for tenacity, looked beyond conventional distribution channels to drive our Toblerone Chocolate business. He identified the link between Toblerone's Swiss heritage and that of the restaurant chain, Swiss Chalet. Gary sold the idea of a free Toblerone with turkey meals during the busy Christmas period. Sales increased by millions of bars . . . and that offer continued for six years, until Kraft lost the business to Lindt. How's that for an unsung hero's adding value?

Paul, a salesman, was the sales department's answer to Ronnie. Paul wore the company colors on and off the job. A CEO couldn't ask for a better soldier on the battlefield. Paul set the standard for cultural values within the organization. He laughed a lot and made hard work, fun. That's important, especially when a business or an industry slips into an economic downturn.

Each year, a group of Jacobs-Suchard employees partook in a one-week Outward Bound team-building excursion into the wilderness. Although Gail, an accounting clerk, was fighting breast cancer, and we all knew it, she volunteered, claiming she was well enough to endure the hardships of a challenging trek in the mountains, but in truth, she desperately wanted to be a part of it. As it turned out, on the final day of that expedition, the ten women on the trek hauled Gail to the top of the world (the mountain's summit) on a makeshift stretcher. She asked that they keep her secret. Within the year, Gail was gone. It would be ten years before one of her teammates tearfully shared this inspirational story of courage with me. You can imagine my reaction. To this day, I cannot repeat that story without a tear in my eye.

No one is an average Joe. Not Ronnie, not Bruce, Gary, Paul, and certainly not Gail. These folks are a company's most valuable players, the unsung heroes. Every leader ought to treat them as such.

Sea Level Simplicity of the "To Do" List

In successful "do less, better" companies, simplicity and focus touch every department and every employee. That's not to say that people don't run up against a heap of tasks that suppress their motivation as well as their productivity. If not rectified over the long term, stress materializes and well-intentioned, talented people succumb to the curse of spending more time "doing" and less time "thinking."

No matter where you are in an organization, the "to do" list can be a valuable tool. But its effectiveness is in direct proportion to the number of items on the list. The daily or weekly "to do" list is developed at sea level, not in the strategic stratosphere. You need one. Your CEO needs one. The president of the United States needs one.

The content of the list and how you work your way through it are the factors critical to the list's effectiveness—you have to come to terms with this before you input into the newest, greatest time-management app.

Know what is essential. Know what to delete from your screen, and when to move on. Know what will bring the greatest return for your effort. Yes, there are menial tasks that we all have to do. If they consume 75 percent of your day, prioritize the other 25 percent. You are still marching to Pareto's principle. Some people set up their lists according to operational and strategic projects. Some differentiate by the value of the task. Some establish goals based on what they can do really well. For example, should a blogger go for quantity or quality of posts? Is a daily post that's been slapped together in a half hour better than a weekly post of insightful, engaging content that might take days to research and write? The answer depends on the blogger's objectives and his or her working style.

When I was at Suchard, one of the marketing managers made a request to hire an extra brand manager. I gave him credit for his courage; he was well aware of my distaste for adding employees. He said his project list had reached a point that precluded him from doing the kind of job he wanted to do. He believed that the recruitment of one individual would make all the difference. I asked him to update his project list and organize it, beginning with the most important and ending with the least important projects. The following day, he brought me the list.

We discussed the projects, and when satisfied that I understood the twenty or so items on his page, I scratched out a third of them. "Stop working on these," I said. "Do you think you can manage the rest without that brand manager?"

Of course he could. Okay, I've simplified the interaction, but not the part about scratching out a third of the projects. News of that symbolic act spread through the company's management group like a wild bush fire. It would be a long time before another incremental hiring request came from the marketing department.

HR and the CEO: Joined at the Hip

When Suchard's Board of Directors promoted me to CEO, they strongly suggested that I align myself with my next-door neighbor in the C-suite. The advice proved excellent, and for the rest of my days in the corner office, I was joined at the right hip with an outstanding finance executive by the name of Dieter Weiskopf, who is now the CFO of Lindt & Sprüngli, the world's leading chocolatier. My regret is that I did not free up my other hip for Human Resources (HR), a group of eager young managers at the rear of the departmental pecking order.

I must admit that my alumni of the coffee and confectionery world would be the first to tell you that marketing occupied a prime piece of the left hip. Of course, my excuse was that I came up through the marketing management ranks. Yes, we were a marketing-driven company, and yes, my mind was consumed with marketing and strategy. But marketing wizardry alone did not make the organization sing. That tribute goes to the exquisite and enthusiastic melodic rhapsody performed by the entire orchestra. Behind the scenes of the competitive battlefield, my glee club (the HR department) made culture their top strategic priority. At center stage, the principles of the cultural strategy (we called it the credo) that hung on the walls of the offices and the plant were practiced by the leadership team.

Good or bad, CEOs determine the corporate culture. During my era, I was competitive, action oriented and results driven. It is no coincidence that these principles and behaviors became those of the employees. I'll explain it this way: at the outset, we recruited for the right cultural fit—attitude first, skills second. The desired cultural characteristics were monitored and measured, annually. Our superior financial results supported this style of modus operandi. In other words, "the way we do things around here" worked. Could I have done more if HR had been attached to that other hip? There is no doubt.

With declining loyalty and greater job hopping in the business environment of the twenty-first-century, it is critical that CEOs partner with the most senior human resource executive. There are four good reasons for this.

Firstly, HR's most important role is to influence the CEO on the culture itself. This is especially important in "revolving door" environments where multinationals make a habit of inserting up-and-comers into senior management roles in foreign countries and smaller business units. In some organizations, such as Walmart and P&G, the cultures are so well defined and so well ingrained that the new executives seldom institute major cultural change.

Secondly, HR ensures an effective system to pinpoint high-potential talent and probable successors. Walmart and P&G are also excellent succession planners. By the time an executive rises to the top, he or she will have spent several years within the organization. The CEO designate will be a "believer" in the culture that makes his or her company great. And if that culture is one of leading change, then that CEO better make change.

Thirdly, an adept HR executive is the CEO's window. HR can be an excellent radar screen for "reading the tea leaves" among the workforce. This is step one toward improving and/or maintaining organizational health. The individual should be on top of changes to business plans and how they are being accepted. Key to success is the ability to instill trust at all levels. The "window" begins to close when HR become the cops. Be wary of that.

Fourthly, a strategic human resources team can be instrumental in helping the CEO (and other C-suite executives) experience leadership's greatest sense of gratification—encouraging, cultivating, and allowing human beings to reach their full potential, both personally and professionally.

Never has the strategic value of the HR team been more important than in the knowledge economy. Take a look at the companies that enjoy persistent success. Often, they have a "way," a distinctive culture that works for them. The custodian of the "way" is the company president and the chief human resource officer. Try to comprehend the magnitude of instilling and protecting a desirable culture in a global enterprise of 53,000 employees and revenues of $60 billion. Larry Page and his "chief cultural officer" must be doing something right. Google ranked first in 2007, 2008, 2012, and 2013 on *Fortune* magazine's "best companies to work for" list. They also earned $12 billion in net income in 2013.

Why the Board of Directors Should Give a Damn about Culture

Wall Street likes anything that increases shareholder value, but they aren't fans of my "do less, better" philosophy. Boards, equally interested in shareholder value, tend to share the view of bigger is better. The C-suites of companies that have diversified beyond core competencies haven't made those choices on their own. I can hear the conversation between the board and the CEO whom I'll call Peter.

> *Board Member*: "Look, Peter, the stock's been flat for three years. What have you got in the pipeline?"
> *Peter*: "The market's only growing by 2 percent, but we continue to edge up our market share and improve our efficiencies."
> *Board Member*: "Sure, but your competitors are acquiring and growing exponentially. Our stock trend to theirs is dismal. If you can't drive up the business we're in, you better look for another to acquire. It's killing two birds with one stone. Sales go up and synergies bring our operating costs down."
> *Peter*: "If that's what you're asking me to do, I'll draw up an acquisition criterion and bring it to the board for approval."
> *Board Member*: "Can we see it next week?"

Okay, I've simplified this fable, but you get the point. Thankfully, my board never pressured me to diversify. But in all my years of dealing with different characters on the board, not once was I challenged with a question pertaining to the organization's culture. I wasn't surprised in the least. These guys (yep, no women in those days) expected me to run their operation as a dynamic entrepreneurial enterprise. As long as the returns were acceptable, they assumed I was doing a decent job of running the show, and I thank them for that. Their interests were profit, shareholder value, efficiencies, headcount, labor climate, and strategic initiatives. Maybe it was the times—a quarter century ago, culture and values were coming of age. And even though culture is a critical determinant of business performance, I suspect many of today's boards still don't give it the attention it deserves.

Envision Google without innovators, or Zappos cutting corners on customer service. Imagine Whole Foods selling processed foods loaded with saturated and trans-fats. This is difficult for us to do because of the cultural disconnect to what these organizations stand for.

Founders infuse corporate values. In the early days of Zappos, Tony Hsieh asked his employees to help define the company's culture. Ever since, employees have continued to submit a few paragraphs on what Zappos means to them. These submissions are unedited and added to a culture book that is updated annually. Zappos gladly ships this book anywhere in the world at no cost. If you don't want the book, you can take a 60-minute virtual tour and see the culture firsthand. Has the culture at Zappos worked at improving performance? Jeff Bezos thought so. In 2009, Amazon bought Zappos for $1.2 billion.[3] Bezos wanted Hsieh to stay at the helm. In 2013, Zappos continues to amaze in more ways than one under the guidance of this insightful leader.

John Mackey understands culture. In 1986, he instituted a policy whereby any Whole Foods employee can look up the salary and bonus of others, including the top management. Seemingly, if workers understood what types of performance and achievement earned certain people more money, he figured, perhaps they would be more motivated and successful, too.[4] Mackey admits to being constantly questioned about salaries. "People want to know why they aren't earning as much as someone else." Mackey tells them it's because "that person is more valuable. If you accomplish what this person has accomplished, I'll pay you that, too."[5]

When the founders are gone, the culture baton is passed down a long line of chief executives. These men (and more recently, women) are responsible for perpetuating "the way" or making changes, depending on the market environment or the needs of the enterprise. Some do it well. Others do not. Boards can help. The board's primary responsibility is to keep an eye on corporate performance. They are charged with providing perspective and input into the long-term business strategy, imparting strategic direction to management, and identifying risk and overseeing mitigation. I'm suggesting that corporate boards should also foster and monitor culture.

Superb strategy and execution comes from the people within the enterprise. Cultures conducive to inspiring individuals and teams are the ones that bring results. This can be an organization's sustainable competitive edge. Sustainable competitive advantage increases shareholder value. Boards give a damn about shareholder value. Isn't it time boards gave a damn about corporate culture?

Procter & Gamble People

Their brands, their market dominance, their global pervasiveness, their profitability ratios, and their stock market value are

reason enough to elevate P&G to the upper echelon of successful companies over the long haul. Yet, the mystical asset that
distinguishes P&G from everyone else in the corporate world is
their human capital. From 1837 to the present, quality people
have been the pillar of this company's sustainability. To those
who have competed against them, this is not an epiphany.

Consistency of quality people never happens without consistency in leadership. These folks take succession planning very
seriously. Decades ago, at the Leo Burnett Company, I was an
account executive on P&G's Head & Shoulders Shampoo. This
was my first exposure to a short marketing plan. In those days,
you had to get everything onto four pages. If you didn't, your
plan was rejected, and all your colleagues knew it.

Jacobs Suchard liked P&G people. Recruiting them was
always a challenge because they were in great demand. Besides,
our Vancouver location was considered to be "out of the fast
lanes." It was Hugo Powell who taught me a helpful interview
trick. We both knew that the interview process with a P&Ger
was one of the interviewee interviewing the interviewer.

"You have to change that dynamic," Hugo said to me. "Ask
them what makes them think they can survive outside of P&G.
Unlikely they've ever considered that."

This was a good question because it afforded the opportunity for us to promote our entrepreneurial style of management.
We'd firstly reinforce our beliefs in strategy and marketing discipline. From there it was a matter of challenging the candidate
with situations where he or she could not research everything
to death, where he or she would need a creative solution with
less media spending—a gutsy big idea that would scare the hell
out the competition. The approach worked, and several adept
P&Gers joined Jacobs Suchard and went on to illustrious leadership roles.

So, what is it about P&G people and the way they do business
that I so admire?

The character of P&G can be summed up in one word—exploration. Throughout its history, P&G has exemplified a restless and driving spirit to learn and to improve. Notwithstanding blips along the way, there is a dedication to integrity in every area of the business. P&G people have a tremendous trust in each other, but the ultimate judge is in the data, such as market share and productivity. Yes, they are intensely competitive, and they compete with each other, but with fairness that ultimately strengthens everyone. And if anyone should make progress at the expense of others at P&G, it isn't for long.

P&Gers have the ability to disagree, and freely do so. This is because they are intrinsically curious and forever zealous about making the best decisions. After the debate and once the decisions have been taken, they cooperatively move forward toward the common goal.

The competence of the people begins with recruiting discipline. You seldom hear of "water walkers" at P&G, or Walmart, for that matter. That doesn't mean P&Gers aren't bright. They are, and department by department, the organization is stocked with dedicated people who are consistently better than their competitor counterparts.

Inherent in P&G is a challenging work environment. The company is structured in such a way that almost every proposal requires concurrence from a peer. Management is inclined to ask questions rather than give orders. It takes individuals with a lot of confidence in their intelligence and spirit to work happily in this kind of system.

The tenets that stock P&G with outstanding people have existed since day one. The behaviors that I've described were taken from a speech delivered to the employees in 1981 by Owen Butler, then Chair of P&G. In his concluding remarks, Butler said, "the challenge of doubling our business in the next decade should be no more frightening in 1980 than it was in 1930 or in 1880 because, just as the base which we need to double has grown, the resources have also grown. We have more good P&G people to get the job done. I have no doubt that we will take great pride in the results."

For the record, 1980 sales were $10 billion; now they are $84 billion. P&G remains in a class by itself in leadership development earning the number three ranking on *Fortune*'s Global Top Companies for leaders and number two on Hay Group's list for the same category in 2012. In 2013, *Chief Executive Magazine* gave P&G the number one ranking on their Top Companies for Leadership list. Mr. Butler passed away in 1998. He is sleeping very peacefully.

Does a Mentor Have to Breathe?

To most of us, mentors are people of experience and knowledge who help the less experienced advance their careers and/or their education. There are plenty of well-known examples throughout the course of history. Aristotle mentored Alexander the Great, Martin Scorsese mentored Ron Howard, and Freddy Laker mentored Richard Branson. Bill Gates revered the early guidance he received from Ed Roberts, who created the Altair 8800, and later the advice of Warren Buffet on many corporate matters.

Early in my business career, I had the privilege of working under two gentlemen who instilled in me the means by which to build businesses and rise from sales representative to CEO. One of these mentors was brilliantly creative, the other skillfully strategic. Paul Palmer was the man who gave me my first job in brand management. Although I was unqualified for the job, Palmer, one of the most confident human beings I have ever met, saw something in me that I never knew existed. He was convinced that he could draw out my dormant creative abilities and teach me how to become a great marketer. Firstly, he had to teach me how to become a brand manager. Palmer would not allow me to fail. For this, and for infusing in me the everlasting belief in the power of my creative mind, I am forever grateful.

As for my strategic mentor, that would be Hugo Powell. I worked with each of these men for five years. But when I finally reached the corner office, I was alone, and rather than join a presidents' forum, I turned to the periodicals of America's best business schools. *Harvard Business Review* became my favorite management resource. In *HBR*, I had the latest thinking from astute strategists like Michael Porter, Henry Ginsberg, Rosabeth Kanter, and John Kotter. By applying the journal's models to Jacobs Suchard's brands and business units, I was able to identify weaknesses and bring clarity to strategic opportunities. Most importantly, the implications and action steps became an "easy sell" to my management team. Each issue included the views of guest contributors, who tackled sticky, hypothetical scenarios posed by the editor. These executive contributors dealt with the situations differently, and their unique approaches broadened my horizons. This resource is available to leaders and managers of the new economy. Use it.

The mentoring that I have just described concerns itself with helping an individual become better at his or her job or profession. The other kind of mentoring places priority on career advancement. The notion submerged in the definition of career is the opportunity to progress. "Getting ahead" was my father's way of saying it. Notwithstanding politics, nowhere is the premise of upward mobility more prevalent than in today's world of business. More and more people are finding and teaming up with mentors, branding themselves, and carefully managing their careers in order to sprint up the quintessential corporate ladder.

There is nothing wrong with ambition, nothing wrong with aspiring for greater responsibility, and nothing wrong with wanting a bigger paycheck. My discomfort with this kind of mentoring is not the end point; rather, it is the means to that end. Seeking out a mentor, vigilantly branding oneself, and consciously managing a career is all characterized by one undeniable fact—it is all about *you*, whereas in a true leadership environment, mentoring is all about the team. I'd rather mentoring be about us, about the team. Honorable career management has to be anchored in the right values for it to work for the individual and the organization.

Mentoring is a wonderful idea when it is based on helping individuals improve themselves so they become better at what they do. A private coach or a mentor's advice may serve to overcome personal weaknesses. It may also deal with leadership, how to handle an impossible boss, or how to tiptoe through the minefields of a toxic corporate culture. When mentoring turns to "Here's what you can do to stand out from the others," your mentor is doing you and your company a disservice.

Twenty years ago when I was with Kraft working out my employment contract, I saw case after case of Kraft managers prioritizing career management over business management. It was an epidemic. Those who did it well rose to senior positions. These skilled politicians set the example for others, especially their subordinates, who often trotted up the staircase on the boss's coattails. Picture the behaviors that created. I'd be willing to bet these behaviors are still prevalent within the walls of Kraft and Mondelez.

Everyone should take their career seriously, but they should not be doing so on a daily or hourly basis at the expense of the greater good of their colleagues. When you consider making a suggestion or a decision in the presence of senior executives, do you consider the ramifications on your career? If you do, you ought to reassess your values and ethics. If you work for a company where the political animals are rewarded with promotions, you should get the hell out of that company before you become one of them. You owe it to yourself. Stop managing your career and start managing the business.

Business, like life, is a journey, not a destination. There's an abundance of excellent companies out there rewarding the contribution of conscientious team players. When all is said and done, isn't this the way you want to play the game of life?

The Power of Momentum

Going hand and hand with the human capital advantage is a rather perplex intangible known as momentum. Momentum is a strength that keeps on giving. Gamblers in the rush of a hot streak believe in this elusive force. Sports teams go on inexplicable winning streaks, while opponents can't seem to string two wins together no matter how hard they try or how talented their roster. Business isn't all that different. But unlike finite measurements such as income statements, stock prices, or market capitalizations, momentum remains a powerful intangible. Companies short on momentum have a difficult time finding it, and those that enjoy momentum seem to ride the big surf for much longer than they should. Take momentum for granted, and the tide will turn—at first you won't realize that it is gone. Then, all of a sudden, the signposts are everywhere. Storm clouds form, and buckets of rain come pelting down. No matter how hard you work to plug the dike or stop the erosion, reversal is evasive.

When I am playing tennis, I am astutely aware of the power of momentum. I know when I have it and when I have lost it. The realization slammed me in the gut during a tiebreaker that I lost, after building up a seemingly invincible 6–0 lead. As soon as my opponent was at 4–6, I knew I was up to my ears in dung. I knew that this negative attitude was a self-fulfilling prophecy, and yet, I was powerless to change it. Now I play every point as though the tiebreaker is tied at 6–6. Works like a charm (well, some of the time).

Like creativity, momentum costs nothing, but sustaining high growth over the long haul is tough. Winners become losers. Look at Kodak, Blockbuster, Borders, and Nortel. These companies rode the wave of success, only to come crashing down after losing their way. Leaders who have suffered the difficult days of turnarounds and managed to resurrect a business are the ones who think about momentum in strategic terms. They cherish the success factors that lifted them from their corporate cesspool. Most will continue to leverage these factors with unabashed zeal. If innovation and creativity brought revival, chances are good that innovation and creativity will remain the cornerstone of their modus operandi for the rest of their careers.

Those of us who endured the Jacob Suchard turnaround in Canada never forgot the agony. Never would we allow ourselves to become complacent. The shareholders benefited handsomely, and so did several young managers who were part of that company during those turbulent times. These talented managers went on to become CEOs or business unit presidents of Nestlé, ConAgra, Campbell's, Anheuser-Busch InBev, Pfizer, Rogers Communications, Electronic Arts, British Columbia Lottery, MeadWestvaco, and Coca-Cola. P&G taught many of these leaders how to do things right. Jacobs Suchard taught them how to do right things.

Chapter 8 Summary

- The glue that binds leadership, strategy, and execution is people—at every level of the organization.
- Pinpoint and honor your unsung heroes. Reducing complexity and bringing clarity to a company bring clarity to their purpose.
- Competitive intangibles are the source from which competitive advantage flows or goes. Human capital is the means and the end.

- Prioritize project lists. More projects run the risk of more people. Fewer, better people dealing with fewer, better projects is the name of the game.
- The strategic value of human resources has never been more important. Culture is the strategy in the new economy.
- Boards give a damn about shareholder value. When a leader successfully links corporate culture to shareholder value, the board will give a damn about culture.
- Stop managing your career and start managing the business. You'll arrive at the same endpoint the old fashioned way.
- Momentum, like creativity is a powerful resource that costs nothing.

CHAPTER 9

Regrets...I've Had a Few

I n chapter 1, I alluded to the fact that if I had a second chance, I would have done a few things differently in my role as a chief executive. I have two categories of regrets—one is cultural, and the other is strategic. For starters, I would have injected more fun into a corporate atmosphere that was intensely (and necessarily) competitive, but needlessly serious.

For all intent and purposes, I treated everyone the same, justifying this behavior as fair and equitable leadership. Unknowingly, I expected my leadership team to adjust to my personality, my "black and white" way of doing things—the barefisted "get it done," no bullshit philosophy. In hindsight, this inconsideration was lazy leadership because I had neglected to filter the intensity or seriousness of my temperament at that particular time. The CEO afterlife suggests I should have taken more care and paid better attention to the unique personalities of each of my direct reports; some obvious adaptations would surely have made their on-the-job lives less stressful and more fulfilling. Now, this is where the rubber hits the road. Even though I have that regret, is it possible that this more caring leadership style would have made any difference to Jacob Suchard's business performance? I would love to answer that question in the affirmative, but in all honesty, I believe it would not have made a difference.

After reading Walter Isaacson's authorized biography of Steve Jobs, I drew the same conclusion with regard to Apple's performance under a leader who lacked sensitivity and compassion. Of Jobs, the *Atlantic Magazine* put it this way: "Apple's founder and CEO could be a cruel and nasty guy. He was also the greatest chief executive of our time. Don't go thinking those two things are related."[1] Being mindful of how you lead in conjunction with getting the job done is the moral of this reflection. You don't have to sacrifice your time, your intensity, your drive, or your high expectations to unleash the sensitivity that dwells within you but seldom percolates to the surface. This isn't the "what to do"; rather, it's the "how to do it." Unlike business strategy, where "doing right things" trumps "doing things right," the reverse is true when it comes to human capital.

My strategic misstep has to do with Howard Schultz and Starbucks. Back in the late eighties, our Zurich head office was very interested in pursuing the emerging specialty coffee retail sector in North America. For decades, they had competed in Germany and Austria against Tchibo, a premium coffee brand distributed through Tchibo stores and thousands of freshness depots in bakeries and confectionery outlets. I shared Zurich's enthusiasm, but argued that our management team was inexperienced in retailing know-how. I suggested we stick to our manufacturing and marketing knitting, but also that we investigate attaining retail expertise through an acquisition of a chain of specialty coffee shops. This is how I came to meet Howard Schultz.

At the time, Howard was looking for investors to help him expand Starbucks from Seattle to the major markets of Canada and the United States. I travelled to Seattle to tour some stores with Howard, and over the course of the day, we chatted about each company's respective cultures, and exchange thoughts on how we might work together.

The prospect of hooking up with Starbucks in its infancy was incredibly exciting. Without getting into too many details, we were looking at an investment by Jacobs Suchard that would have given us a sizable minority stake in Starbucks and the exclusive rights to Starbucks in the Canadian market. The next step in the process was to put Howard in front of our largest shareholder, Klaus Jacobs. At a Jacobs Suchard board meeting, Howard made his case for the investment, but Klaus wasn't interested in the opportunity. He said he didn't think Starbucks would ever make a profit because of never-ending expansion costs. The irony in this contention was that Klaus Jacobs, like Howard Schultz, was a successful entrepreneur.

Of course, there was more to it. At the time, Klaus was caught up in the mania of global branding. He wanted to be in the retail coffee business, but the brand had to be Jacobs. This wasn't going to fly with Howard. The rest is history. Starbucks became the biggest coffee company in the world. Jacobs Coffee is now one of many Kraft brands, the vast majority of its sales limited to Germany and Austria.

My mistake was in not zealously seeking a small retail chain to acquire—a dozen stores would have been adequate to teach us the ins and outs of the coffee retail model. Even if we had changed the brand name to Jacobs, we would have been in the game early enough to be a force within the budding specialty coffee sector. Frankly, it was easier to stick to the proverbial knitting. We were growing, building brand equity, increasing profits, and keeping the Zurich head office out of our backyard. I should have known better. I became snarled in the paradigm of "Red Ocean" thinking—continuing along in an existing market and playing by the competitive rules that determine growth or decline in market share. The specialty coffee market was set to explode. Howard Schultz had figured it right.

Nonetheless, the operation I continued to run performed exceedingly well until the acquisition by Kraft. The company boasted 13 uninterrupted years of earnings growth, coffee leadership in Canada, a profitable North American Swiss Water decaffeinated operation, a premium line of European chocolates, and annual sales per employee of more than a half million dollars. Kraft recognized the strategic health of this company's brands and the opportunities for overhead synergies. Although saddened by the sale, the takeover afforded me a fulfilling CEO afterlife.

Learn to Teach, Teach to Learn

When I decided to become a blogger in matters pertaining to leadership, strategy, and marketing, I realized that I'd better figure out how to improve my relevancy. Without familiarizing myself with twenty-first-century business and the products and services that did not exist when I was a CEO, I'd be of questionable value. My crash course in catch-up taught me more than I ever would have imagined. I am once again "thinking business" and enjoying the rush of discovering the ideas and innovations of today's new dogs.

Learning the ways and means of several successful techs was my most illuminating lesson. I also discovered that innovation and entrepreneurship was not dead in traditional industries. Chobani Greek Yogurt and the "cult" energy drink market made sure of that. Every marketer engaged in consumer products or services ought to examine Red Bull's strategies and innovative promotional properties. Do that and you can't help but think differently about your own brand and the social universe of today's consumers. Even if you are snagged in the bureaucracy net of an old economy organization, you cannot ignore the fact that great ideas create change.

Your idea can change a company. It can also change you. Believe me, there is nothing like a big idea and its viability to set the framework for how you will lead and manage for the rest of your career.

Pardon the repetition, but as I near the conclusion of this book, I want to reinforce ten critical tricks that I learned in the trenches and battlefields of a 40-year business career, and in the reflective serenity of my afterlife.

1. *Complexity in a company is a cancer.* Keep it simple. Strive for focus in everything you do. Be prepared to take a pass on opportunities that will compromise your core strategy.
2. *Strategy is more important to business than ever.* The ever-increasing pace of business and the endless list of options at a

In chapter 1, I alluded to the fact that if I had a second chance, I would have done a few things differently in my role as a chief executive. I have two categories of regrets— one is cultural, and the other is strategic. For starters, I would have injected more fun into a corporate atmosphere that was intensely (and necessarily) competitive, but needlessly serious.

For all intent and purposes, I treated everyone the same, justifying this behavior as fair and equitable leadership. Unknowingly, I expected my leadership team to adjust to my personality, my "black and white" way of doing things—the barefisted "get it done," no bullshit philosophy. In hindsight, this inconsideration was lazy leadership because I had neglected to filter the intensity or seriousness of my temperament at that particular time. The CEO afterlife suggests I should have taken more care and paid better attention to the unique personalities of each of my direct reports; some obvious adaptations would surely have made their on-the-job lives less stressful and more fulfilling. Now, this is where the rubber hits the road. Even though I have that regret, is it possible that this more caring leadership style would have made any difference to Jacob Suchard's business performance? I would love to answer that question in the affirmative, but in all honesty, I believe it would not have made a difference.

After reading Walter Isaacson's authorized biography of Steve Jobs, I drew the same conclusion with regard to Apple's performance under a leader who lacked sensitivity and compassion. Of Jobs, the *Atlantic Magazine* put it this way: "Apple's founder and CEO could be a cruel and nasty guy. He was also the greatest chief executive of our time. Don't go thinking those two things are related."[1] Being mindful of how you lead in conjunction with getting the job done is the moral of this reflection. You don't have to sacrifice your time, your intensity, your drive, or your high expectations to unleash the sensitivity that dwells within you but seldom percolates to the surface. This isn't the "what to do"; rather, it's the "how to do it." Unlike business strategy, where "doing right things" trumps "doing things right," the reverse is true when it comes to human capital.

My strategic misstep has to do with Howard Schultz and Starbucks. Back in the late eighties, our Zurich head office was very interested in pursuing the emerging specialty coffee retail sector in North America. For decades, they had competed in Germany and Austria against Tchibo, a premium coffee brand distributed through Tchibo stores and thousands of freshness depots in bakeries and confectionery outlets. I shared Zurich's enthusiasm, but argued that our management team was inexperienced in retailing know-how. I suggested we stick to our manufacturing and marketing knitting, but also that we investigate attaining retail expertise through an acquisition of a chain of specialty coffee shops. This is how I came to meet Howard Schultz.

At the time, Howard was looking for investors to help him expand Starbucks from Seattle to the major markets of Canada and the United States. I travelled to Seattle to tour some stores with Howard, and over the course of the day, we chatted about each company's respective cultures, and exchange thoughts on how we might work together.

The prospect of hooking up with Starbucks in its infancy was incredibly exciting. Without getting into too many details, we were looking at an investment by Jacobs Suchard that would have given us a sizable minority stake in Starbucks and the exclusive rights to Starbucks in the Canadian market. The next step in the process was to put Howard in front of our largest shareholder, Klaus Jacobs. At a Jacobs Suchard board meeting, Howard made his case for the investment, but Klaus wasn't interested in the

- Prioritize project lists. More projects run the risk of more people. Fewer, better people dealing with fewer, better projects is the name of the game.
- The strategic value of human resources has never been more important. Culture is the strategy in the new economy.
- Boards give a damn about shareholder value. When a leader successfully links corporate culture to shareholder value, the board will give a damn about culture.
- Stop managing your career and start managing the business. You'll arrive at the same endpoint the old fashioned way.
- Momentum, like creativity is a powerful resource that costs nothing.

CHAPTER 9

Regrets... I've Had a Few

opportunity. He said he didn't think Starbucks would ever make a profit because of never-ending expansion costs. The irony in this contention was that Klaus Jacobs, like Howard Schultz, was a successful entrepreneur.

Of course, there was more to it. At the time, Klaus was caught up in the mania of global branding. He wanted to be in the retail coffee business, but the brand had to be Jacobs. This wasn't going to fly with Howard. The rest is history. Starbucks became the biggest coffee company in the world. Jacobs Coffee is now one of many Kraft brands, the vast majority of its sales limited to Germany and Austria.

My mistake was in not zealously seeking a small retail chain to acquire—a dozen stores would have been adequate to teach us the ins and outs of the coffee retail model. Even if we had changed the brand name to Jacobs, we would have been in the game early enough to be a force within the budding specialty coffee sector. Frankly, it was easier to stick to the proverbial knitting. We were growing, building brand equity, increasing profits, and keeping the Zurich head office out of our backyard. I should have known better. I became snarled in the paradigm of "Red Ocean" thinking—continuing along in an existing market and playing by the competitive rules that determine growth or decline in market share. The specialty coffee market was set to explode. Howard Schultz had figured it right.

Nonetheless, the operation I continued to run performed exceedingly well until the acquisition by Kraft. The company boasted 13 uninterrupted years of earnings growth, coffee leadership in Canada, a profitable North American Swiss Water decaffeinated operation, a premium line of European chocolates, and annual sales per employee of more than a half million dollars. Kraft recognized the strategic health of this company's brands and the opportunities for overhead synergies. Although saddened by the sale, the takeover afforded me a fulfilling CEO afterlife.

Learn to Teach, Teach to Learn

When I decided to become a blogger in matters pertaining to leadership, strategy, and marketing, I realized that I'd better figure out how to improve my relevancy. Without familiarizing myself with twenty-first-century business and the products and services that did not exist when I was a CEO, I'd be of questionable value. My crash course in catch-up taught me more than I ever would have imagined. I am once again "thinking business" and enjoying the rush of discovering the ideas and innovations of today's new dogs.

Learning the ways and means of several successful techs was my most illuminating lesson. I also discovered that innovation and entrepreneurship was not dead in traditional industries. Chobani Greek Yogurt and the "cult" energy drink market made sure of that. Every marketer engaged in consumer products or services ought to examine Red Bull's strategies and innovative promotional properties. Do that and you can't help but think differently about your own brand and the social universe of today's consumers. Even if you are snagged in the bureaucracy net of an old economy organization, you cannot ignore the fact that great ideas create change.

Your idea can change a company. It can also change you. Believe me, there is nothing like a big idea and its viability to set the framework for how you will lead and manage for the rest of your career.

Pardon the repetition, but as I near the conclusion of this book, I want to reinforce ten critical tricks that I learned in the trenches and battlefields of a 40-year business career, and in the reflective serenity of my afterlife.

1. *Complexity in a company is a cancer.* Keep it simple. Strive for focus in everything you do. Be prepared to take a pass on opportunities that will compromise your core strategy.
2. *Strategy is more important to business than ever.* The ever-increasing pace of business and the endless list of options at a

leader's disposal necessitate clarity of purpose. Differentiate your business and your brands from the rest of the pack with unique services or customer benefits. Leverage those differences to get ahead. Reinvent yourself to stay ahead.

3. *Creativity is the last great bargain in business.* Institutionalize it within your modus operandi and mind-set. This is difficult for big company people to understand or appreciate because many have been raised in environments where "spend your way out of it" is a panacea. Creativity is the key to the smaller competitor's success. With the emergence of social media and online commerce channels, including mobile, the influence of creativity is immeasurable.

4. *Culture is the strategy.* Look at Zappos. Look at Google. Look at Twitter. These companies are characterized by challenging and motivational work, meaningful purposes, great working environments, and the ability to grow professionally.

5. *Peer beyond the current fiscal year.* Develop strategies that define the future and guide the actions you take today. But don't misinterpret short-term problems as strategic. They may hinge on strategic issues, but for the most part, smart, well-executed tactics can overcome short-term problems and edge an organization closer to its strategic vision.

6. *Life is a journey, not a destination.* So is business. I did not fully appreciate the essence of this cliché until I left the corner office and discovered so many meaningful interests and hobbies that were unrelated to business. Enjoy the journey and don't wait until your career is over to discover the hidden "you."

7. *Balance work life and home life.* Hug your kids. They grow up so much faster than you think. Sure, there are times when you'll have to put in the long hours away from your loved ones. But don't tell me you can't work smarter. Working smarter facilitates family time. The business will not suffer—especially when you do less, better.

8. *Business is exciting.* Okay, so there are more roadblocks to contend with than in my day—government meddling, environmental regulations, cheap foreign labor and low-priced imports. But look at the opportunities—online marketing, social media, niche products and services, specialization, new markets. For the strategic and creative mind, the list is endless.

9. *"Greed is good" is becoming "greed for green."* Entrepreneurs invest where they see bright economic prospects. Saving the planet has become very good business. In the renewable energy market, global investments have increased from $33 billion in 2004 to $211 billion, seven years later. Think green. Think corporate social responsibility.

10. *Love what you do.* In the world of business, this means living your passion. My niche happened to be brand marketing. Now that I'm out of business, my passion is writing. This book represents the first fruit of my efforts. My next goal is finding a publisher willing to take a chance on a fiction manuscript written by a rookie novelist.

Business Proverb Bullshit

Generally speaking, proverbs are known for their valuable insights, but some have been so overused that they no longer evoke contemplation. When I searched online for content on business proverb "lies and mistruths," I was amazed by the breadth and depth of the digital library. Well-intentioned myths apply to business in general, as well to as specific industries, start-ups, and the flourishing digital world. And while proverbs do come and go, the most recurring are ingrained as truth—no one dares question them.

Who in their right mind is going to take issue with the importance of customers, shareholders, and strategic based decision-making? Certainly not I, but I'll gladly break the paradigms of three pet peeves, which like a bad rash, won't go away.

1. *The customer is always right.* This is crap. There's not a salesman out there who hasn't heard a customer spew an unsound reason for not buying something. Depending on the circumstance, when the customer is wrong, you have two choices: sacrifice your sense of right and wrong (as well as your pride) by keeping your mouth shut, or diplomatically and reverently make the correction with rational reasoning. In due course, customers will respect you for your honesty and your service principles. If they don't...well, what can I say? You can sleep well at night knowing you gave them what they needed, which was better than what they wanted. In extreme circumstances, you might lose the customer by doing that. Maybe that's not such a bad idea. Surely the time has come for companies and sales executives to modify this idiom around improved customer service mantras. How about "service wins the game" or "there is no traffic jam along the extra mile of customer care." Never in the history of business has there been so much attention to customer service. Never has customer service been so poor.

2. *The CEO's first responsibility is the shareholders.* This is also crap. No question, business can't exist without shareholders and, yes, increasing shareholder value is one of the CEO's most important responsibilities. But the shareholder does not come first. Employees come first, customers come second, and shareholders come third. Bear in mind that "third" does not mean "last." This notion is based on the premise that happy employees make for happy customers, and happy customers make for happy shareholders. I've been criticized for my naiveté on this concept, but I am not backing off. Illustrating the concept as a circular treadmill of satisfaction is a marvelous way of pacifying the shareholder or board member who raises an eyebrow at the thought of not being numero uno, but rather, one of three connected

stakeholders. CEOs who put their employees first are the most successful at building businesses and are the most fulfilled, personally. I can vouch for that in the CEO afterlife. I remember people and triumphs, not profits. But if I had failed to deliver profits, I would not have been in the C-suite long enough to generate a fruitful environment in which my employees could realize their potential.

3. *The decision was made for strategic reasons.* I can't cry foul to this because bad decisions *are* made for strategic reasons. Here's the hitch: the strategy stinks. My blood boils at the ongoing reliance upon the word "strategy" to justify stupidity from the executive row. When there isn't a logical explanation for an ill-conceived top-down decision, messengers use "strategy" as a crutch. They say, "I don't like it either, but from what I'm told, Mr. Bighead made the call for strategic reasons." In more cases than not, if Mr. Bighead's decision was dumb, then so too was Mr. Bighead's strategy.

So what do you do the next time you encounter one of these mistruths in hallway conversation? If you are the boss, you holler "bullshit" at the top of your lungs. On the other hand, if your boss is the one discharging the crap, then your most astute career move is to count to ten under your breath and visualize the smiling faces of your kids.

Envision Your Epitaph

If you are already in the C-suite, or aspiring to get there, I suggest you take a moment to contemplate your CEO epitaph. Do you want to be remembered as Jack Bighead or Andy Goodfellow?

I'll begin by describing the afterlife of Jack Bighead: a master dealmaker, the tenacious Mr. Bighead believed a good deal was one in which the other side got screwed. Throughout his highly successful career, he created hundreds of millions in shareholder value by acquiring, downsizing, and selling companies. This hard-driving CEO never let anything stand in the way of his insatiable quest for profit, nor has he any regrets of sacrificing family time for the good of the business and the shareholders. On missing the graduations of all four children, Mr. Bighead said, "Comes with the territory. At least each of 'em got a spanking new sports car." From his glorious manor on the Boca Raton coast, he contemplates his decadent future with his third wife, Mercedes, a former Las Vegas showgirl.

By contrast, there is the epitaph of Andy Goodfellow: if you met him in the street, you'd never know that the soft-spoken Mr. Goodfellow was a successful, results-oriented CEO. He was the type of leader who never talked about himself; he was interested in you. "People first" was his modus operandi. Perhaps that's why his employees always gave that "extra mile" for the customer. With great pride, he watched the men and women who worked under him go on to fulfilling careers as masters of their chosen craft. As for his retirement, Mr. Goodfellow is excited. He plans to spend more time with his wife of 41 years, his three children, and eight grandchildren. "I'll also be busy heading the Goodfellow Foundation, the charity that helps people help themselves," he said.

There may be many styles of leadership, and some will hinge on the state of the business. But if you don't want your CEO epitaph to resemble that of Jack Bighead, be aware of those you touch along the way. Notwithstanding the incessant trials and tribulations, there is every opportunity to lead with honor and do some good with the power of the C-suite while you occupy it.

Those of you who have followed my blog have an idea of how I'm spending my time in retirement. Beyond my recreational life (weapons of choice being a tennis racquet and a golf club—on a good day I use both), I'm loving the challenge of writing, and I'm every bit as goal oriented as I was 30 years ago. Fortunately,

I don't take myself as seriously as I did in my business days. I no longer fret about my insecurities or fear the political animals lurking in the hallowed hallways of the Zurich head office.

Looming retirement can be awfully daunting to a CEO, especially to those who define themselves by their jobs. Think about the personal and behavioral characteristics of the stereotypical CEO. They are

- performance driven,
- energetic and tenacious,
- passionate and disciplined,
- visionary,
- resourceful.

In addition, they enjoy their leadership role and the power that goes with it. Imagine how difficult it is for these folks to keep their egos in check. These five characteristics, plus ego and power, are the very traits that motivate ex-CEOs in their afterlife. Many find satisfaction using their influence to help others. They get behind philanthropic causes with all the zeal and determination they exerted while rising to the top of the corporate ladder. Former CEO of sports apparel maker Russell Corporation, Jack Ward, puts his time and money into helping inner-city kids.[2] Warren Staley (Cargill) supports Habitat for Humanity with a hammer, a saw, and a wallet.[3] GE's Jack Welch divides his time consulting with companies, traveling, golfing, lecturing at the Massachusetts Institute of Technolog, writing, and donating time and money to business education.[4]

But not every CEO follows this path. Some find happiness pursuing interests that evaded them during the demanding years in the executive suite. At one time I worked for a hard-driving chap who was prematurely pushed out of the corporate cockpit, a golden parachute strapped to his back, and no hobbies or interests beyond business. Worried for his mental well-being, his wife bought him paint, canvas, an easel, and lessons.

Painting wasn't the answer. But the notion of artistic discovery inspired my former boss. He embarked on creating life-size, caricature stone sculptures of people he knew. He became an excellent sculptor and a much happier man than he ever was in the executive suite. You could see it in his eyes whenever he spoke of his work and his desire to improve. He glowed.

There are so many wonderful examples of former CEOs finding exhilarating second lives in their golden years. And in each and every case where the retiree has unleashed a new passion to help others, there is an endless line of beneficiaries from students to sick kids, from young entrepreneurs to lovers of art (as was the case with my former boss). To those of you nearing the end of an era, do not fret. A world of challenge and discovery fills the souls of your retired brethren. Join the campaign.

The lessons in this book on the big idea of strategic sacrifice apply to every leader and every organization, big or small. Good leaders, good strategies, and good corporate values need not cost a penny more than bad leaders, bad strategies, and bad cultures. Sure, my heyday as a business leader occurred during an era of less complexity. So I ask you—if well-considered sacrifices selected on their ability to create or fortify competitive advantage worked in a less complicated business world, why wouldn't it work now?

Acknowledgments

It is customary for authors to acknowledge those who made their book possible. While I am grateful to my literary agent and the good people at Palgrave Macmillan in this regard, I want to use this opportunity to express my appreciation to those who helped me navigate through a challenging terrain of a long career.

Early in the game, three bosses established the foundation for my success. Paul Palmer gave me my start in marketing, and despite my struggle to measure up to his expectations, he wouldn't allow me to fail. Rupert Brendon introduced me to the power of creativity in the world of advertising. Hugo Powell nurtured my strategic mind and bolstered my competitive spirit.

At Jacobs Suchard (Nabob), a diverse team of outstanding individuals made the David versus Goliath story a twentieth-century business story. The notables were Roger Barnes, Steve Bolliger, Grant Campbell, Jim Collins, Mike Coltart, Bob Crockett, Kurt Dyck, Brian Elliot, Helmut Emmert, Steve Fox, Gary Gover, Ron Habijanac, Elaine Hemingway, Cam Janzen, Don Macdonald, Bruce McKay, Sandra Morrison, Valerie Samson, Ron Sangster, Laurel Smith, Eric Sorensen, Terri Spagnuolo, Boyd Stevens, Laura Sullivan, Terry Taciuk, Pierre Taillbois, Diane Teer, Vincent Timpano, David Twentyman, Susan Vann, Joe Weber, Dieter Weisskopf, Judy Wilkinson, and Glenn Wong.

After Suchard, several other individuals emerged as great clients, colleagues, and confidants: Peter Blackwell, Don Chisholm, John and Lotte Davis, George Fleischmann, Dean Francis, Casey Houweling, Neil McDonnell, Vic Poleschuk, Lewis Rose, A.J. Slivinski, Jim Thorne, and Justin Thouin.

Thank you all for the memories.

Notes

1 Accept the Short-term Pain

1. Global Simplicity Index. http://www.simplicity-consulting.com/research _items/global-simplicity-index-2/.
2. Roberto Goizueta (1931–1997). *New Georgia Encyclopedia*. http://www .georgiaencyclopedia.org/articles/business-economy/roberto-goizueta -1931-1997.
3. Al Ries. *Focus: The Future of Your Company Depends on It* (Harper Business, 1996), 74.
4. Roberto Crispulo Goizueta. *Gale Encyclopedia of Biography*. http://www .answers.com/topic/roberto-goizueta.
5. MarketWatch.com. http://www.marketwatch.com/investing/stock/ko /financials.
6. MarketWatch.com. http://www.marketwatch.com/investing/Stock/PEP /financials.
7. Bloomberg Business News. "Company Reports; Anheuser-Busch Shutting Its Eagle Snack-Food Unit," February 8, 1996, http://www.nytimes.com /1996/02/08/business/company-reports-anheuser-busch-shutting-its-eagle -snack-food-unit.html.
8. Dana Mattioli. "Tyson Wins Bid Against Itself," *Wall Street Journal*, June 9, 2014, http://online.wsj.com/articles/tyson-foods-nearing-deal-for-hillshire -brands-1402314461.
9. Venessa Wong. "Starbucks Gets Ready to Go from Tall to Venti in China." BusinessWeek.com, November 1, 2013, http://www.businessweek.com /articles/2013-11-01/starbucks-gets-ready-to-go-from-tall-to-venti-in-china.
10. Dale Buss. "Domino's Global Growth Feeds Pizza Chain's Rising Success," March 9, 2013, http://www.forbes.com/sites/dalebuss/2013/03/09/dominos -global-growth-feeds-pizza-chains-growing-success/.
11. Wikinvest.com. http://www.wikinvest.com/stock/Campbell_Soup_Company _(CPB).
12. MarketWatch. http://www.marketwatch.com/investing/stock/cpb/financials.
13. James Manyika, Michael Chui, Brad Brown, Jacques Bughin, Richard Dobbs, Charles Roxburgh, Angela Hung Byers. "Big Data: The Next Frontier

for Innovation, Competition, and Productivity," http://www.mckinsey.com
/insights/business_technology/big_data_the_next_frontier_for_innovation.

14. Avinash Narula. "The 80/20 Rule of Communicating Your Ideas Effectively," Wikipedia http://en.wikipedia.org/wiki/Pareto_principle.

15. University Alliance. "Wal-Mart's Keys to Successful Supply Chain Management," http://www.usanfranonline.com/wal-mart-successful-supply -chain-management/. [Name of website]

16. P&G Brands. http://en.wikipedia.org/wiki/List_of_Procter_&_Gamble _brands.

2 The Steel and Steal of Strategic Sacrifice

1. "Most Executives Don't Think Their Company's Strategy Will Lead to Success," Stragegy&, June 4, 2014, http://www.strategyand.pwc.com /global/home/press/display/coherence-profiler-results?gko=52a77.

2. Eric Savitz. "Wal-Mart's Growing Push into Digital," Forbes.com, November 18, 2012, http://www.forbes.com/sites/ericsavitz/2012/11/18 /interview-walmarts-growing-push-into-digital-commerce/.

3. Allistair Barr. "Walmart.com CEO Joel Anderson to Step Down," *Wall Street Journal*, June 9, 2014, http://online.wsj.com/articles/walmart-com-ceo -in-the-u-s-joel-anderson-to-step-down-company-memo-1402348383.

4. Exxon Mobil Mission. http://exxonenergy.com.yeslab.org/html/ourcoAbout Index.htm.

5. Staples Mission. http://www.staples.ca/ENG/Static/static_pages.asp?pagename =soulmain.

6. Venkatesh Rao. "Why Amazon Is the Best Strategic Player in Tech," Forbes.com, December 14, 2011, http://www.forbes.com/sites/venkateshrao /2011/12/14/the-amazon-playbook/3/.

7. John Cook. "Jeff Bezos on Innovation," GeekWire.com, June 7, 2011, http://www.geekwire.com/2011/amazons-bezos-innovation/.

8. John Revill. "Nestle Has Patent for Nespresso System Revoked," euroinvestor. com, October 11, 2013, http://www.euroinvestor.com/news/2013/10/11 /nestle-has-patent-for-nespresso-system-revoked/12530756.

9. Chris Bryant and Henry Foy. "Porsche to Build Cars in entirety outside Germany for First Time," FT.com. March 19, 2014, http://www.ft.com /intl/cms/s/0/5022b050-aeb7-11e3-aaa6-00144feab7de.html#axzz3Axe 1LRFW.

10. Michelle Russell. "Kraft Foods Group Insists Innovation Improving," Just-Food.com, February 19, 2014, http://www.just-food.com/news/kraft -foods-group-insists-innovation-improving_id122218.aspx.

11. Oliver Nieburg. "Mondelez Sets Global Vision," ConfectioneryNews.com, September 10, 2014, http://www.confectionerynews.com/Manufacturers /Mondelez-sets-global-chocolate-vision.

12. Max Nisen. "The 15 Companies that Frustrate Americans the Most," BusinessInsider.com, December 26, 2013, http://www.businessinsider. com/companies-with-the-worst-customer-ratings-2013-12?op=1.

13. 2012 Mondelez Annual Report, http://ir.mondelezinternational.com /secfiling.cfm?filingID=1193125-13-73227&CIK=1103982.

3 Your Leadership Reality Check

1. PR Newswire. "Average Tenure of CEOs Declined to 8.4 Years, The Conference Board Reports," April 12, 2012, http://www.prnewswire.com /news-releases/average-tenure-of-ceos-declined-to-84-years-the-conference -board-reports-147152135.html.
2. Eric Savitz. "HP: Maybe They Really Should Get out of PCs (and Printers)," Forbes.com, July 13, 2012, http://www.forbes.com/sites/ericsavitz/2012/07 /13/hp-maybe-they-really-should-get-out-of-pcs-and-printers/.
3. HP 2013 Annual Report, page 41, http://media.corporate-ir.net/media _files/IROL/71/71087/AR-2013-t21sfr/index.html
4. USS Tranquility. http://www.usstranquility.com/.
5. United States Courts. Business Banruptcy Filings http://news.uscourts .gov/bankruptcy-filings-down-fiscal-year-2012.
6. Susan Wojcicki. "The Eight Pillars of Innovation," ThinkWithGoogle. com, July 2011, http://www.thinkwithgoogle.com/articles/8-pillars-of -innovation.html.
7. New Media Trend Watch. "World Usage Patterns & Demographics," http:// www.newmediatrendwatch.com/world-overview/34-world-usage-patterns -and-demographics.
8. Lululemon Manifesto. http://www.lululemon.com/about/manifesto
9. Richard Blackwell. "'I am not the culture of Lululemon,' Outgoing CEO Christine Day Says," TheGlobeandMail.com, July 13, 2013, http://www .theglobeandmail.com/report-on-business/lululemon-is-in-great-shape -says-departing-ceo/article12513015/.
10. The 100 Most Creative People in Business. FastCompany.com. April 27, 2012. http://www.fastcompany.com/3018187/most-creative-people-2012/4-ron -johnson.
11. "Leo Burnett," *Wikipedia*, last modified August 7, 2014, http://en.wikipedia .org/wiki/Leo Burnett.

4 The Urgency for Action

1. BrainyQuotes.com. http://www.brainyquote.com/quotes/quotes/a/andremauro 104357.html.
2. Luxottica website, http://www.luxottica.com/en/about-us/company-profile /facts-and-figures.
3. Warby Parker website, http://ca.warbyparker.com/.
4. Joseph Fry and Peter Killing. *Strategic Analysis and Action*, Canadian Edition, 4th edition, Ontario: Prentice-Hall, 1999.
5. Melodie Warner. "Campbell Soup reports lower profit, sales ," MarketWatch. com. November 22, 2011, http://www.marketwatch.com/story/campbell -soup-reports-lower-profit-sales-2011-11-22.

6. Vivian Giang and Melissa Stanger. The 50 Best Companies to Work for in 2013. BusinessInsidercom, December 12, 2012, http://www.businessinsider .com/the-50-best-companies-to-work-for-in-glassdoor-2013-2012-12? op=1.

7. In-N-Out Not-So-Secret Menu, http://www.in-n-out.com/menu/not-so -secret-menu.aspx.

8. Ron Margulis. "At PLMA Show, a Heyday for Store Brands," CanadianGrocer. com. November 20, 2014, http://www.canadiangrocer.com/top-stories /store-brands-doing-better-than-ever-as-innovations-abound-34669.

9. Goodreads.com, http://www.goodreads.com/quotes/451403-whenever-you -see-a-successful-business-someone-once-made-a.

5   Think Like an Entrepreneur

1. Diana Ransom. "Chobani Yogurt's Success Starts Where a Giant Left Off," Entrepreneur.com. May 25, 2012, http://www.entrepreneur.com/blog /223668.

2. Alissa Figueroa. "Chobani Founder Turns Centuries-Old Greek Yogurt into Billion Dollar Craze," *Rock Center with Brian Williams*, Rock Center, December 12, 2012, http://rockcenter.nbcnews.com/_news /2012/12/12/15866373-chobani-founder-turns-centuries-old-greek-yogurt -into-billion-dollar-craze?lite. 2

3. Gary Hamel and C. K. Prahalad. *Competing for the Future*, Harvard Business Review Press, 1996, p. 28.

4. MarketWatch.com, "2013 EA Financials," http://www.marketwatch.com /investing/Stock/EA/financials.

5. Nitin Pangarkar and Mohit Agarwal. "The Wind behind Red Bull's Wings," Forbes.com, June 24, 2013, http://www.forbes.com/sites /forbesasia/2013/06/24/the-wind-behind-red-bulls-wings/.

6. Ibid.

7. MarketWatch, "2013 Monster Financials," http://www.marketwatch.com /investing/Stock/MNST/financials.

8. Associated Press. "Coca-Cola bets on Energy Drinks with Monster Stake," August 14, 2014.

6   KISS Is Not a Rock Band

1. Ronald D. White. "U.S. Charitable Giving Jumped 13% in 2013," LATimes. com. January 13, 2014, http://articles.latimes.com/2014/jan/13/business /la-fi-mo-charitable-donations-record-2013-americans-20140113.

2. Laura Barnett. "L'Oréal Adverts: Don't Airbrush over the Truth," TheGuardian.com. July 28, 2011, http://www.theguardian.com/lifeandstyle /2011/jul/28/airbrushing-loreal-adverts-jo-swinson.

3. Coke Slogans, *Wikipedia*, http://en.wikipedia.org/wiki/Coca-Cola_slogans.

4. Pepsi Slogans, *Wikipedia*, http://en.wikipedia.org/wiki/Pepsi.

5. Nicole Mezzasalma. "Pernod Ricard Acquires V&S Absolut Spirits," DFNIonline.com. March 31, 2008, http://www.dfnionline.com/article /Pernod-Ricard-acquires-VS-Absolut-Spirits-1856313.html.
6. Gibson YouTube. "The Making of Gibson Guitar," YouTube, September 22, 2006, http://www.youtube.com/watch?v=3vARFwbhLOM.
7. Fender website, http://www.fender.com/.
8. Gibson website, http://www2.gibson.com/Products/Electric-Guitars/Archtop /Gibson-Custom/Citation.aspx.
9. "The Martin Story," Martinguitar.com, http://www.martinguitar.com/guitar -care/care-a-feeding-guide/8-main-site/the-martin-story.html.
10. Robin Grant. "Wieden+Kennedy's Old Spice Case Study," WeAreSocial.net, August 10, 2010, http://wearesocial.net/blog/2010/08/wieden-kennedys-spice -case-study/.

7 Bastions of Branding

1. Bruce Horovitz. "More Than Anything Else, Technology Will Pave the Way for Innovative Change at Starbucks," USAToday.com, April 24, 2013, http://www.usatoday.com/story/money/business/2013/04/24/starbucks -howard-schultz-innovators/2047655/.
2. Corporate Design Foundation. "Interview with A.G. Lafley," CDF.org, http://www.cdf.org/issue_journal/interview_with_a.g._lafley.html.
3. Kellogg's. *2011 Annual Report*. http://www.annualreport2011.kelloggcompany .com/letter.htm.
4. Sam Byford. "Sony Makes First Net Profit in Five Years Despite Falling Demand for Core Products," TheVerge.com. May 9, 2013, http://www .theverge.com/2013/5/9/4314430/sony-2012-fy-earnings.
5. Sony 2012 Annual Report. June 29, 2012, Letter to Shareholders by the CEO. http://www.sony.net/SonyInfo/IR/financial/ar/2012/message/page01.html.
6. John Reynolds. "Profile: Jennelle Tilling, Vice-President of Marketing, UK and Ireland at KFC," MarketingMagazine.co.uk, June 24, 2011, http:// www.marketingmagazine.co.uk/article/1063711/profile-jennelle-tilling -vice-president-marketing-uk-ireland-kfc.
7. Francois Gossieaux. "Brand Positioning Takes on a New Meaning in this Hyper-Social World," AMABoston.org. November 11, 2009, http://connect .amaboston.org/profiles/blog/list?user=symbiotic&page=2.

8 Fewer, Better People Doing Less, Better

1. Barry Jaruzelski, John Loehr, and Richard Holman. "The Global Innovation 1000: Navigating the Digital Future," Strategy&, October 22, 2013, http://www.strategy-business.com/article/00221?pg=all. (formerly Booz & Company).
2. Rosamund and Benjamin Zander. *The Art of Possibility*, Penguin Books, 2000, p. 89.

3. Robin Wauters. "Amazon Closes Zappos Deal, Ends Up Paying $1.2 Billion," TechCrunch.com. November 2, 2009, http://techcrunch.com/2009/11/02/amazon-closes-zappos-deal-ends-up-paying-1-2-billion/.

4. Kim Peterson. "At Whole Foods, Paychecks Are Public," cbsnews.com, March 5, 2014, http://www.cbsnews.com/news/at-whole-foods-paychecks-are-public/.

5. Ibid.

9   Regrets . . . I've Had a Few

1. Tom McNichol. "Be a Jerk: The Worst Business Lesson from the Steve Jobs Biography," TheAtlantic.com, November 28, 2011, http://www.theatlantic.com/business/archive/2011/11/be-a-jerk-the-worst-business-lesson-from-the-steve-jobs-biography/249136/.

2. Henry Unger. "Retired CEO Finds His Calling," ajc.com, January 5, 2010, http://blogs.ajc.com/business-beat/2010/01/05/retired-ceo-finds-his-calling/.

3. Twin Cities Habitat for Humanity, http://www.tchabitat.org/worldofhope/donors/staley/.

4. "Jack Welch," *Wikipedia*, Last modified July 31, 2014, http://en.wikipedia.org/wiki/Jack_Welch.

Index

80/20 rule, 31

Absolut Vodka, 145–6, 149
activists, 59
adversaries, 21, 91
Aero brand chocolate, 49
Ali, Muhammad, 63
Allstate, 167
Amazon
  acquisitions, 188
  brand, 159, 169
  competition, 82, 93
  effect on book retailers, 82
  hustle approach, 100
  innovation, 117, 124
  online business, 22, 39–40
  simplicity and, 22
  strategy, 44–5, 100
  Walmart and, 39–40
  Zappos and, 188
AMEX (American Express), 146, 168
Amy's Kitchen, 28, 120
Anheuser-Busch, 8, 21–3, 89, 172, 196
anticipatory change, 94
Apple, 40, 50, 78, 83, 118, 151, 201
Art of Flight, The (film), 126
Art of Possibility, The (Zander), 179
AT&T, 51

baby boomers, 16, 151–2, 154
Bank of America, 51
bankruptcy, 62, 64, 89
Barclays, 49
beer market, 22–3, 89, 128, 144, 171–2
  see also Anheuser-Busch; Carlsberg;
    Miller Genuine Draft

Bezos, Jeff, 45, 118, 157, 159–61, 188
  see also Amazon
Bird, Larry, 115
Birds Eye, 23
Black Label, 171
BlackBerry, 82, 92–3, 95
Blockbuster, 196
BMW, 146, 168
boards of directors, 17, 28, 107–8
boldness, 78, 84–6, 93
Bolthouse Farms, 28
Borders, 196
BP (British Petroleum), 74, 84
Brach's, 7
brands
  Amazon, 159, 169
  brand awareness, 91
  brand management, 10, 38, 115, 119,
    123, 135, 137–42, 145, 150, 162, 166,
    173, 184, 192
  Church of Brand, 143–6
  creating brands, 51–2, 126–7, 137–41
  diversification and, 26–7
  entrepreneurship and, 126–8
  image and, 93–4, 107, 119, 125, 141–3
  leadership and, 69, 73, 77, 82
  longevity and, 147–9
  luxury brands, 90
  marketing and, 39, 96–7, 111
  old brands, 149–51
  P&G, 32, 138, 153, 160, 173
  private label and, 101–2
  profit and, 39
  social media and, 137, 143–4, 147, 172–4
  specialization and, 21, 23–4
  Starbucks, 42, 46, 158–9, 168

brands—*Continued*
strategy and, 4
termination of product lines and, 5–6,
16, 32
value and, 6, 47
vision and, 139, 158, 161
Branson, Richard, 118, 157–8, 160, 192
brick and mortar, 39–40, 66, 69, 113
Brin, Sergey, 65
Bristol Myers, 123, 150–1
British Columbia Lottery Corporation,
105, 178–9, 196
Brylcreem, 150
budgets, 76–7, 82, 106, 111, 125, 141, 153
Budweiser, 144, 171–2
Buffet, Warren, 192
Burnett, Leo, 85
Butler, Owen, 191–2

Cadbury, 51, 69
Calpino, Barry, 48–9
Campbell's Soup, 8, 21, 26–9, 61, 95, 98,
160, 163, 196, 213
Carlsburg, 171
catchphrases, 144, 165
see also slogans
celebrity, 61, 146, 149, 157
Champion spark plugs, 170
Chanel, 90, 142
charity, 62, 138–40, 165, 182, 209
Charter Communications, 51
chief financial officer (CFO), 30
chief marketing officer (CMO), 8, 23, 78,
142, 161
chief operating officer (COO), 78
chief technology officer (CTO), 78
China, 24, 68
Chisholm, Don, 169
Chobani, 66, 94, 112–14, 120, 153, 173,
204
Chunky Soup, 29
Cialis, 152
Cirque du Soleil, 73, 159
clarity, 3, 19, 40, 43–4, 48, 62, 70, 85, 105,
162, 164, 181, 193, 196, 205
Clearasil, 32
Cline, Elmer, 170
clout, 40, 49, 51–2, 56, 90, 113, 128
clutter, 66, 140, 147, 157
Coach, 90

Coca-Cola, 17–21, 24, 29, 68, 123, 126,
128–9, 137, 144, 164, 168, 196
Colombia Coffee Growers, 157
Columbia Pictures, 19
Combe Inc., 150–1
complacency, 91–2, 117, 128, 196
complexity, 8–9, 13–18, 21, 25–33, 38, 46,
53–4, 59, 65, 69, 76, 105, 137, 144,
157–8, 178, 196, 204, 211
ConAgra, 21–3, 196
contraction, 54, 56
Corante, 173
Corning, 124
Cosby, Bill, 157
Cote D'Or, 7
coupons, 81–2, 93
credo, 107, 185
Crisco, 32
Crisis Change, 94–5
Crisis Curve, 94–5, 108
crisis management, 62, 74–7, 98
culture
board of directors and, 187–9
brand and, 111, 159, 167–8
CEOs and, 185–7
complexity and, 30, 33
credo and, 107
innovation and, 48–9, 117–18, 120–1,
123–4, 126–7, 131
leadership and, 73–80
manifestos and, 72–3
simplicity and, 151
small businesses and, 52–6
Starbucks and, 42
turnarounds and, 93, 98
urgency and, 91

da Vinci, Leonardo, 63
Danone, 51, 112–14
Darwin, Charles, 63
Day, Christine, 73
De Beers, 167
Declaration of Independence, 70
defensiveness, 65
DieHard batteries, 170
differentiation, 23, 40, 47, 73, 81, 85, 103,
106, 125, 127, 135–7, 148, 152, 154,
164, 168, 173–4, 184, 205
dismissals, 5, 59, 74, 89
Disney, 73, 118–19, 146

Doetsch Grether, 150
Domino's Pizza, 25
Dossier Creative, 169
Dove, 170
Dow Jones, 61
Drucker, Peter, 48, 104
Duncan Hines, 23, 32
Duval Guillaume Modem, 171

Eagle Snacks, 23
"early bird gets the worm" theory, 127
"easily definable," 63
eBay, 124, 169
EBITDA (earnings before interest, taxes,
     depreciation, and amortization), 15
Edison, Thomas, 63
Electronic Arts (EA), 121, 196
Eli Lilly, 152
emotion, 5, 15–17, 33, 41–3, 65, 70, 72, 83,
     99, 126, 128, 143, 145–6, 158, 164,
     166–71, 174
energy drinks, 125–8, 159
     see also Monster Energy; Red Bull
Enrico, Roger, 20–1, 29
Entrepreneur Magazine, 112
entrepreneurial thinking
     corporations and, 120–3
     "going green" and, 129–31
     innovation and, 116–20, 123–4
     overview, 111–12
     seeing unseen, 114–16
     small-business ethic, 112–14
     younger companies and, 123–4
     zig and zag energy, 124–9
entry-level jobs, 123
Eukanuba, 32
Exxon Mobil Corporation, 41, 52

Facebook, 100, 106, 147, 153, 172
face-to-face interaction, 69
Fact Toothpaste, 150
farsightedness, 86, 93, 102
Fast Company, 123
Faulkner, William, 9
FedEx, 116
Fender, 146–9
Focus: The Future of Your Company
     Depends on It (Ries), 19
Folgers, 32, 115
Forbes, 44, 172

Ford, Henry, 116
Ford Motor Company, 124
Fosters, 171
Franklin, Ben, 63
Fry, Nick, 93

Gates, Bill, 65, 115, 192
General Electric (GE), 14, 124, 210
General Foods, 51
General Mills, 28, 167
generalists, 17, 20–6, 31, 33, 47, 53, 71, 90
genetically modified organism (GMO), 51
Gibson Guitars, 146–9
Ginsberg, Henry, 193
glassdoor.com, 101
Goizueta, Roberto, 18–19, 21, 29
Google, 45, 65, 93, 98–100, 106, 117, 124,
     150, 153, 172, 187–8, 205
Gossieaux, Francois, 173
greed, 129, 206
green businesses, 129–31, 206
greenhouse farming, 70–1, 168
Gretzky, Wayne, 114
Grey Goose, 142

Häagen-Dazs, 169
Hanes, 23
Hansen, Rick, 182
Harley-Davidson, 119, 152, 172
Harvard Business Review, 193
Hawking, Stephen, 13
Hay Group, 192
Hayes, Geoff, 145
Hayward, Tony, 74
Head & Shoulders shampoo, 190
Hershey, 113
Hillshire Brands Company, 21, 23
Hirai, Kaz, 162
Houweling, Casey, 71–2, 129, 168
Houweling's, 70–2, 129–30, 168
Howard, Ron, 192
HP (Hewlett Packard), 61–2, 95
Hsieh, Tony, 118, 157, 159–61, 188
     see also Zappos
human resources (HR), 185–7
hustle and, 101–2

Iams, 32
iconic brands, 52, 121, 152, 163–5, 170
inaction, 117

Indianapolis International Balloon Race, 170
ingenuity, 48, 111, 131
initial public offerings (IPOs), 100
In-N-Out Burger, 101
innovation
    Amazon and, 117, 124
    culture and, 48–9, 117–18, 120–1, 123–4, 126–7, 131
    entrepreneurial thinking and, 116–20, 123–4
    Kraft and, 48–9
    P&G and, 124
    vision and, 115, 117
intangibles, 177, 195–6
InterBrew, 23, 89
iPad, 115
Ipana toothpaste, 150
iPhone, 82, 115
iPod, 115, 170
Isaacson, Walter, 201
Ivy School of Business, 93

J.C. Penney, 78, 93, 95
Jackson, Michael, 29, 159
Jacobs, Klaus, 202–3
Jacobs Suchard, 4, 7, 18, 48, 50–1, 69, 75–7, 89, 95–6, 113, 125, 142, 166, 182, 184–5, 190, 193, 196, 201–2, 213–14
Jell-O, 157
Jif, 32
Jobs, Steve, 83–4, 115, 160, 201
    see also Apple
Johnson, Ron, 78
Johnson's Foot Soap, 150
"Just Do It" campaign, 144–5, 167
    see also Nike

Kanter, Rosabeth, 193
Keebler, 161
Kellogg's, 160–1
Kelsen Group, 28
Key Business Indicators (KBIs), 106
key performance indicators (KPIs), 60
KFC, 20, 157, 168
"kill your darlings," 5, 9, 29–30, 32, 62
Kindle, 45
    see also Amazon
King, Martin Luther Jr., 70

KISS (keep it simple, stupid), 136, 139–40, 152–4
    see also simplicity
Kiwi, 23
knee-jerk reactions, 82
Knight, Phil, 157–8, 160
Kodak, 120–1, 162, 196
Kotter, John, 193
Kraft
    acquisitions, 4, 6–7, 51, 166
    Chobani and, 66, 112
    divisions, 69
    innovation and, 48–9
    Jacobs Suchard and, 4, 6–7, 18, 48, 96–7, 143, 166, 203
    management, 194
    Mondelez and, 49, 51–2, 69, 122
    Toblerone and, 182
Krating Daeng, 125
    see also Red Bull

Labatt Breweries, 89, 171
Lafley, A. G., 160
Laker, Freddy, 192
Laliberté, Guy, 159–60
layoffs, 74
leadership
    boldness and, 84–5
    CEOs and, 83–4
    future and, 67–70
    manifestos and, 70–3
    new economy and, 65–7
    overview, 59–62
    rough times and, 80–3
    strategy and, 77–80
    ultimate test of, 73–7
    vision and, 62–5
LensCrafters, 90
Leo Burnett Agency, 85, 160, 190
Levi Strauss, 124
Levitt, Theodore, 135
Lindt, 182, 185
L'Oréal, 143, 146, 149
loyalty, 5, 69, 71, 79–80, 113, 150, 152, 186
Lululemon Athletica, 72–3
Luxottica, 90–1

Mackey, John, 157, 159–60, 189
manifestos, 70–3, 86
Maple Leaf Foods, 8

Marketing Imagination, The (Levitt), 135
Mars, 32
Martin Guitar Company, 149
Mateschitz, Dietrich, 125, 127, 159–60
  see also Red Bull
Maurois, Andre, 89
Maxil, 150
Maxwell House, 115, 166
Mayer, Marissa, 98
McDonald's, 146, 161, 164
McKinsey Global Institute, 30
MeadWestvaco, 196
Mercedes-Benz, 47, 148
"Michael Jackson: The Immortal World
  Tour," 159
Michelob, 171
Microsoft, 65, 100, 124
Mike's Hard Lemonade, 169
Milka, 7, 48
Miller Genuine Draft, 171
mission statements, 40–3, 72, 117
Mission to the Edge of Space (film), 126
momentum, 195–7
Mondelez, 49, 51–2, 69, 122, 194
Monsanto, 51
Monster Energy, 127–9, 137
Montana, Joe, 115
Morin, Joseph, 63
movies, 144, 158, 162
Müller, Matthias, 47
Mum Deodorant, 150

Nabisco, 51, 69
Nabob Foods, 4, 6–7, 48, 143, 166–7, 213
National Basketball Association (NBA), 115
National Football League (NFL), 61
National Hockey League (NHL), 114
Nestlé, 4, 6, 46, 49, 93, 172, 196
Nielsen, 101
Nike, 73, 118–19, 143–5, 158, 164, 167
nimbleness, 14, 31, 50–1, 56, 91, 100–1, 153
Nintendo, 169
non-governmental organizations (NGOs), 50
Nortel, 196
Noxema, 32

Oakley, 90
Old Spice, 153
Oracle, 124
organic foods, 28, 32, 120

Outward Bound, 182
Oxfam, 138

Pacific Soups, 28
packaged goods industry, 6, 93, 122, 125,
  138, 160
packaging, 6, 102, 113, 138, 148, 166, 168,
  171
Page, Larry, 45–6, 65, 187
Palmer, Paul, 192
Panera Bread, 42
Pareto's Principle, 31, 184
Patagonia, 111
Pearl Vision, 90
PepsiCo, 19–21, 24, 29, 68, 83, 126, 128,
  137, 144
Pernod Ricard, 145–6
Peters, Tom, 85, 117
Pfizer, 8, 152, 196
Pinnacle Foods, 23, 136
Pinterest, 153, 173
Pizza Hut, 20
Plum Organics, 28
Porsche, 47, 142
Porter, Michael, 193
Powell, Hugo, 89–90, 190, 193, 213
Prada, 90
pride, 118–19, 179–80, 207
Pringles, 32, 161
private labels, 22, 46, 55, 101–2, 135
Procter & Gamble (P&G)
  brand management, 138, 153, 160, 173
  cosmetics and, 143
  culture, 186, 190–2, 196
  food industry and, 18
  innovation and, 124
  nimbleness and, 51
  old brands and, 150–1
  "pruning" of divisions, 32–3
  SBUs and, 14, 18, 32–3
  social media and, 173
produce industry, 54, 71–2, 130
productivity, 30, 60, 69, 71–2, 107, 178,
  183, 191
Progresso, 28
Puri, Bharat, 49

qualitative strategy, 48–9
quantitative strategy, 48–9, 83, 107
Quiller-Couch, Arthur, 9

Radio Shack, 93, 162
Ralcorp, 21
Ralph Lauren, 90
Rao, Venkatesh, 44
Ray-Bans, 90
Reactive Change, 94–6
Red Bull, 49, 125–9, 137, 159, 204
Red Bull Street Kings (film), 126
"Red Ocean" thinking, 203
retail market
    Amazon and, 22, 39–40, 82
    coffee, 5, 96, 202–3
    culture and, 111
    distributors and, 128
    eyewear, 90
    food, 66, 71, 101
    hustle and, 101–2
    J.C. Penney and, 78
    Luxottica and, 90
    musical instruments, 148
    online, 22, 39–40, 68, 111
    strategy and, 39–40
    Walmart and, 31–2, 39–40
    Warby Parker and, 90
Rich Corporation, 136–7
Ries, Al, 19, 128
Roberts, Ed, 192
Rock Center (TV show), 66, 113
Roddenberry, Gene, 64
Rogers Communications, 196
ROI (return on investment), 151
Roig, Kaitlin, 74
Rosenfeld, Irene, 122
Russell Corporation, 210

sacrifice, 179–81
Sara Lee, 21, 23
SC Johnson, 23
Schultz, Howard, 23, 42–3, 84–5, 115–16, 158, 160, 202–3
Scorsese, Martin, 192
Scully, John, 83
SeaPak, 136–7
Senft, Riley, 139–40
shareholders
    acquisitions and, 19, 23, 143, 196, 202
    CEOs and, 59, 67, 124, 207
    company performance and, 3, 27, 40, 59–61
    leadership and, 3–4, 59, 67–9, 74–5, 85, 89

reactive change and, 95
value and, 23–4, 95, 107, 138, 177, 187–9, 197, 207
Shark Tank, 119
Shiseido, 143
Siemens AG, 123
simplicity
    baby boomer market and, 151–2
    brand and, 137–41, 143–6
    longevity and, 146–9
    marketing management performance review, 141–3
    old brands and, 149–51
    overview, 135–7
    social media and, 153–4
    "to-do" lists and, 183–5
slogans, 43, 119, 126, 140, 144, 147, 150, 165–8, 174
    see also catchphrases
Slovakia, 47
Smith, Harry, 66, 113
social media
    authenticity and, 114
    brand and, 137, 143–4, 147, 172–4
    budget and, 82, 112
    creativity and, 205
    customers and, 115
    entrepreneurship and, 120
    growth of, 122
    marketing and, 112, 114–15, 141
    sacrifice and, 6, 10
    small businesses and, 112, 131, 153–4
Softique Bath Oil, 150
solar energy, 129–30
Sony, 162, 170
Southern Comfort, 169
Special K, 160–1
specialization, 17–19, 31, 181, 206
Standard & Poor's 500, 177
Staples, 40–2
Star Trek, 64
Starbucks
    acquisitions and, 46
    author's work with, 8, 23
    branding, 158–9, 168
    Canada and, 202
    China and, 24
    competitors, 115–16
    culture, 73
    customer model, 96

Day, Christine and, 73
decaffeinated coffee, 96–7
growth, 42–3, 115–16, 202–3
investors, 202
product additions, 116, 158–9
Schultz, Howard and, 23–4, 42, 202–3
specialist strategy, 24–5
success, 23–4, 27, 42–3
Ten Peaks and, 96–7
Stewart, Martha, 115
strategic business units (SBUs), 14
strategic initiatives, 16, 82, 95, 103, 107,
    188
strategy
Amazon and, 44–5, 100
big/small companies and, 48–53
complexity of, 43–7
focusing, 53–5
mission statements and, 40–3
overview, 37–40
retail and, 39–40
Starbucks and, 24–5
vision and, 45, 60, 78, 106–7, 125, 146,
    205
Step Into Action, 140, 165
Suchard
    see Jacobs Suchard
Sullenberger, Chesley "Sully," 74
Sunglass Hut, 90
supremacy, 102
Swanson frozen dinners, 27
Swiss Water, 48, 96–7, 203
SWOT (strengths, weaknesses,
    opportunities, threats) analyses, 104

Taco Bell, 20
tactics, vs. strategy, 38–40, 55, 103
Tchibo, 202
television, 61, 119, 140, 144, 150, 153
Ten Commandments, 70
Ten Peaks Coffee, 97
Thomas, Gibu, 40
Tide Detergent, 39
Tiffany, 90
Time Warner, 51
Toblerone, 7, 48, 113, 182
Tombstone Pizza, 51
Trader Joe's, 116
Trig Deodorant, 150
Trump, Donald, 84, 122

turnarounds, 3, 5, 17, 50, 61, 67, 89, 93–9,
    196
Twitter, 106, 147, 153, 172, 205

Ulukaya, Hamdi, 66, 112–14, 122
Unilever, 21, 143, 172
United Way, 138
unsung heroes, 181–3, 196
UPS, 123
urgency
    culture and, 91–2
    hustle approach, 100–2
    overview, 89–93
    strategic naysayers, 102–4
    strategy and, 104–8
    turnarounds and, 93–8
    Yahoo and, 98–100
US Airways, 74
US Small Business Administration (SBA),
    112

V&S Group, 145–6
Van Houten Chocolate, 7
Viagra, 152
Virgin, 158
vision
    boldness and, 85
    brand and, 139, 158, 161
    charity and, 139–40
    competition and, 130
    culture/credo and, 107
    entrepreneurial, 53, 115
    greatness and, 62–5
    innovation and, 115, 117
    KBIs and, 106
    leadership and, 15, 60, 62–6, 86, 99,
        102, 111, 158, 210
    manifestos and, 70–1, 73
    marketing and, 137, 157
    mission statements and, 40–2, 122
    strategic, 45, 60, 78, 106–7, 125, 146, 205
Vitalis Hair Tonic, 150
Vlasic Pickles, 23, 27
Volkswagen Beetle, 47, 145, 170

Walkman, 9, 170
Wall Street Journal, 98
Walmart, 31–2, 39–40, 43, 118, 124, 186,
    191
Warby Parker, 90, 94

Ward, Jack, 210
Weiskopf, Dieter, 185
Welch, Jack, 210
Wheaties, 167
Whitman, Meg, 61–2
Whole Foods, 117, 159, 188–9
Wikipedia, 67
Williams, Brian, 66
Winfrey, Oprah, 115
Wonder Bread, 170
word of mouth, 112, 125, 131, 170

World Wildlife Fund (WWF), 138
World's Most Powerful Brand list, 172
Wrangler Jeans, 160

Yahoo, 98–100
Yoplait, 112, 114

Zander, Benjamin, 179–80
Zander, Rosumund, 179
Zappos, 111, 159, 169, 188, 205
Zuckerberg, Mark, 115